ACTION ON PLASTIC

c l a u d i  w i l l i a m s
## Small Steps to Less Waste

stories to
inspire
change

QUICKTHORN

# Foreword

The topic of plastic pollution has been an incredible gateway for the public to engage with environmentalism. Plastic, in particular damaging single-use plastic, is prolific in all of our lives. We all use plastic every day in some form or other. Despite our amazing Plastic Free Communities programme, the refill movement and other attempts at reducing waste, plastic water bottle production continues to rise, another 8 per cent this year, and the long-term forecast is for single-use plastic production to accelerate. And, this was true even before the pandemic hit and we saw a new wave of PPE and plastic pollution smothering planet ocean.

However, rather than lose hope, now is the time for us all to redouble our efforts. This will be the decade of environmental action.

Faced with the accelerating impacts of climate change and runaway global heating, we must call on our world leaders and global industry to take action. In this book, people from the Stroud community urge us to also look for solutions closer to home. By making and repairing things for ourselves, we can avoid excessive packaging and waste of all kinds. The Stroud district became one of our Plastic Free Communities in 2020 and in these pages, you will meet some of the people at the forefront of this local initiative. The simple, practical solutions and skills shared here are transferrable and can be replicated in any town and any country anywhere. Individual, everyday actions can become collective action and make a real difference in the world.

Keep up the good fight. Every action you take is important.

### Hugo Tagholm
*Chief Executive, Surfers Against Sewage*

# Contents

# Introduction

It is clear to all but those who refuse to see, that the global environment is deteriorating at a dramatic and increasing rate. The air we breathe, the water we drink, the soil we plant our crops in and the food we eat are all being compromised by our current societal systems and the unsustainable lifestyles we live. The vast majority of scientists agree that we are in the midst of a mass extinction of our own making and it is known that many current life forms will be extinct by the end of this century. The impacts of climate change are already being felt everywhere, especially in the global South, and as the reality of our unpreparedness comes to light, eco anxiety about what the future might look like now grows.

The proliferation of plastic over the last few decades plays a role in the lives of nearly all humans around the globe and exemplifies our impact on the environment. Rather than being a global crisis of its own, plastic pollution is now understood as a serious hazard, which is accelerating climate change. While we might imagine that plastic pollution starts with what we do with the products after we've used them, we are now waking up to the fact that there are serious consequences throughout the life cycle of plastic, from production to disposal. Starting with the extraction and transportation of fossil fuels such as oil and natural gas needed for plastic production, the harmful process continues at the vast industrial plants that release a slew of toxic emissions into surrounding communities. Notably, the ways in which plastic pollutes the earth are often less obvious than other forms of pollution; according to a recent study led by Dr Ian Kane at the University of Manchester, published in the journal *Science*, one of the greatest threats currently comes from the microfibres that are released by synthetic clothing with each wash and now make up the majority of microplastic lying on the seabed.

We know that processes such as these threaten the stability and biodiversity of whole ecosystems, both on land and in the ocean, from the bottom to the top of the food chain. We also know that the ways in which we currently address these issues are insufficient; a very small percentage of some plastics is recycled, delaying rather than avoiding final disposal. The rest ends up being burned, put in landfills or transported back to nature through other means. To put a figure on it, if current production and waste management trends continue, roughly more than 12,000 million tonnes of global plastic waste will be in landfills or in the natural environment by 2050.

We must press governments for better regulation, introduce meaningful producer responsibility, overhaul recycling systems and change our lifestyles. Indeed, despite popular debate, lifestyle change and systemic change do not compete, and it is outdated thinking to assume that our individual

> **'...our individual choices act as signals to those around us about what we deem important; to our friends, families and communities around the globe as well as the producers in polluting industries who depend on us for their existence.'**

actions are insignificant or irrelevant. In addressing global crises, we should bear in mind that those who have been successful in galvanizing social action, such as Greta Thunberg, have insisted on individual change – and modelled it – while advocating systemic change.

Concerns about animal welfare, fair trade, sustainability and our impact on the planet are not just political topics, they are related to the lifestyle choices we make. When we choose how we sustain ourselves, we are participating in an arena of competing claims for what and how much society should produce, how it should be used and at what cost. The potential for positive impact in this sphere can be understood when we recognise that our actions take place in an interconnected social reality where a single act can be seen by many and inspire similar action. As such, our individual choices act as signals to those around us about what we deem important; to our friends, families and communities around the globe as well as the producers in polluting industries who depend on us for their existence. Given this reality, we can appreciate that our everyday actions each contain the potential to shift social norms and drive self-perpetuating institutional changes.

Times of upheaval are always times of radical change. The Covid-19 pandemic is a crisis that has interrupted our habits and made their shortcomings visible, highlighting the need to scale down human activity and the merits of a simplified lifestyle: less consumption and less reliance on consumer convenience. It has also demonstrated the potential of collective action and the power we have to adapt our lives and encourage others to follow, proving that we can affect major changes to help ourselves and for the greater good. The pandemic is a chance to reset and envision the future, emphasising the solutions that make us true citizens: looking out for each other, taking only what we need, supporting local solutions and reviving the art of cooking, gardening and making and repairing. In short, it has shown us a more sustainable way to share life on earth.

*Oliver Williams, 2020*

Sources

- www.theguardian.com/environment/2019/may/15/single-use-plastics-a-serious-climate-change-hazard-study-warns
- www3.weforum.org/docs/WEF_The_New_Plastics_Economy.pdf (p.7)
- link.springer.com/article/10.1007/s10584-019-02463-0
- www.theguardian.com/environment/2020/apr/30/microplastics-found-in-greater-quantities-than-ever-before-on-seabed-currents-hotspots
- www.storyofplastic.org/learn-every-step
- advances.sciencemag.org/content/3/7/e1700782
- science.sciencemag.org/content/368/6495/1140

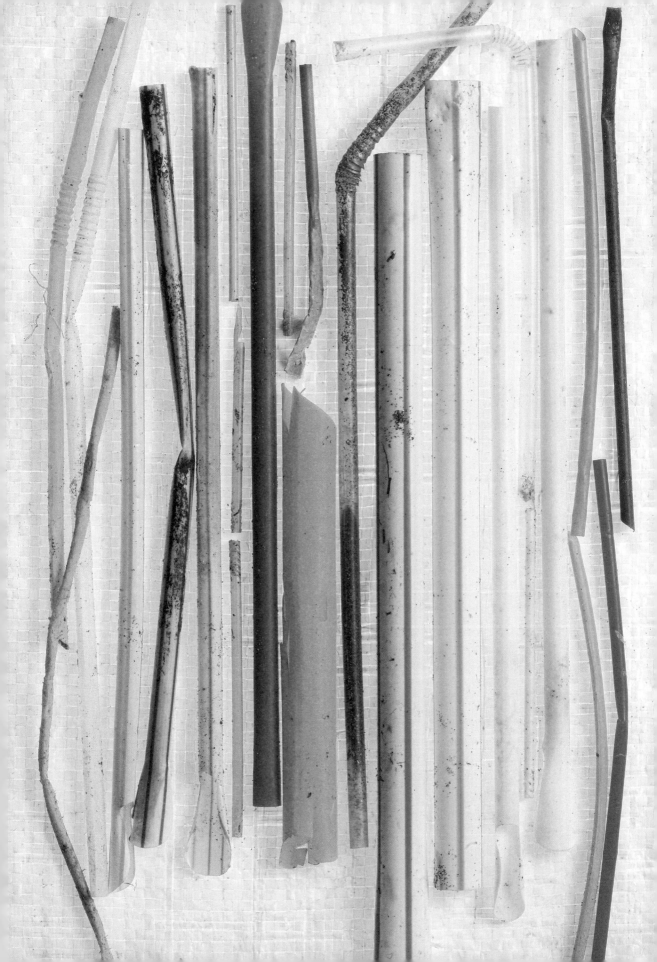

# Plastic Free Stories

# Our plastic free year and beyond

On the first of May 2016 my family and I made a pledge to stop buying anything made of plastic or packaged in plastic for one whole year. It was an experiment to see to what degree we could eliminate plastic from our daily lives. How difficult would it be? How much would we need to give up? Would it be more expensive? How would it change our lives? At the time, plastic pollution was not a widely discussed topic. Single-use plastic was a relatively unknown term and supermarkets had yet to embrace the idea of customers bringing their own containers to the store.

My husband and I had long been frustrated by the increase of plastic in all areas of our lives and the lack of information on recycling – unwrapping the weekly shopping left us with masses of unrecyclable packaging which went straight into the bin. It troubled me that from the minute I awoke to turn off the alarm clock, right through to brushing my teeth last thing at night, my hands seemed to be touching plastic. The previous summer we had found ourselves swimming in a 'plastic soup' off a pristine beach in Mallorca, which had deeply disturbed me. The plastic was under the water's surface, long pieces of faded plastic film and other nondescript items, eerily wrapping around my legs like seaweed. Back home I began to search for information on plastic in the oceans and stumbled on story upon story of beaches choked by plastic litter, sea creatures entangled in discarded fishing nets and starving sea birds, their guts bulging with plastic debris. It was heartbreaking.

The morning I read about 13 dead sperm whales beached on the north coast of Germany with stomachs full of plastic, I knew that I had to do something. I suddenly realised that I was part of the problem: I was accepting all this plastic in my life. I was in the supermarkets every week, moaning about the increase in packaging but buying it nevertheless. I wanted to stand up and say 'no more'. This was also the morning that I decided to take a one-year, no plastic pledge and thankfully my lovely family decided to join me.

What followed was an utterly absorbing, fascinating and rewarding journey that became a permanent lifestyle change, causing ripples that touched our family, friends and community. The changes we have made are not immediately apparent to the naked eye. To see the impact on our household one would need to scrutinize the contents of our bins, go through kitchen and bathroom cupboards, check the fridge and the freezer, the laundry room, garden shed and garage. One would need to come shopping with us, watch us cook and clean, prepare for celebrations such as birthdays or Christmas and come with us on business trips and holidays. Only then one might notice an almost total absence of that

'An almost total absence of that
ubiquitous, man-made material that
has found its way into every corner
of modern life, no matter how and
where we live.'

'Avoiding plastic required determination and creativity: we had to look back to how things used to be done before plastic was invented, then put a modern spin on it.'

ubiquitous, man-made material that has found its way into every corner of modern life, no matter how and where we live.

There seemed to be very little information on how to live without plastic either in books or online, which really surprised me. Over the course of the year we had to make sacrifices and put a lot of work into finding plastic-free solutions. Before long though, we started to get the hang of it and I began to write a blog (www.pfree.co.uk) to chronicle our journey and provide information and practical advice for other people who might want to embark on a similar journey. We wanted to tell people how rewarding it was once we got over the biggest hurdles and tell them about the many unexpected benefits of our new lifestyle. The day that *Blue Planet* made people in the UK sit up and take notice of plastic pollution in the oceans, thousands of people landed on our little-known blog.

We learned early on that the use of the most common alternatives to plastic, such as biodegradable and compostable plastic, metal, glass, cardboard, bamboo and cotton, are the cause of many unintended consequences and are often more carbon hungry than plastic itself. The best solution was to buy unpackaged or not buy at all. 'Do I really need this' became a mantra. We became forensic in detecting plastic in hidden places: the lining of food tins and drink cans, in Tetra Pak cartons, teabags, toiletries, household cleaners, in the

glues, inks and laminates of printed packaging, in recycled toilet paper, till receipts, clothing, shoes, zips, buttons... the list became endless and it became nearly impossible to buy anything new. Avoiding plastic required determination and creativity: we had to look back to how things used to be done before plastic was invented, then put a modern spin on it. We began to take a real interest in learning how to repair broken items, mend our clothes and make things for ourselves. We were surprised and delighted to find that many of the solutions we were seeking were readily available locally, at repair cafés and up-skilling workshops.

Perhaps one of the most impactful insights we had during the year was that plastic facilitates excessive consumption. Alongside technological and medical advances, plastic also makes it possible to mass-produce products cheaply and fill supermarket shelves with affordable food shipped from around the globe all the year round. Convenience, choice, affordability and instant gratification of our every desire have become the hallmarks of modern life. We are pacified by the possibility of improved recycling and a circular economy and we applaud new innovations such as compostable and biodegradable plastic. In the meantime, we are steadily heading into a climate crisis. Refusing to buy anything plastic brought me face to face with my own levels of consumption. It was hard to give up so many of the things I liked having – favourite cosmetics, blueberries in the middle of winter, crisps, ready-made-meals at the end of a long day at the office. Once we had begun to learn the true cost of plastic to the environment, to wildlife and even to our own bodies, it was impossible to 'un-learn' and there was no going back.

The number of metric tons of plastic produced every year is staggering, beyond comprehension and governments are woefully unprepared for the safe disposal of the toxic waste that plastic turns into. Only a small percentage of plastic is recycled. In 2017 a comprehensive report looking at all plastic produced since 1950 estimated that 8,300 million metric tons (Mt) of virgin plastics have been produced to date. As of 2015, approximately 6,300 Mt of plastic waste had been generated, around nine per cent of which was recycled, 12 per cent was incinerated, and 79 per cent was accumulated in landfills or the natural environment. We are only beginning to scope out the problem with production, use and disposal of plastic polymers. There are new studies, research findings and reports on plastic pollution coming out at an alarming rate. We now know that nanoparticles of plastic can be found everywhere, from the deepest ocean floor to the highest mountain glaciers. Plastic particles are raining down on us from the air and are travelling up through the food chain. Even so, the plastics industry is looking to expand and oil extraction for plastic production, including from shale fracking, already equals the amount of oil extracted for the entire aviation sector.

## How we did it

At first it was very difficult to source even the most basic day-to-day items such as pasta, rice, toilet paper or toothpaste. Processed and convenience food in particular is often double and triple packed in plastic to keep it fresh or to extend its shelf life. My first trip to the supermarket with my usual shopping list was a disaster. I returned home with only three items and the realisation that this was going to be a difficult task. We signed up to a local milk delivery in glass bottles and began to shop more regularly at the farmers' market, farm shops, butchers and bakers. The way we managed to balance our busy lives with the demands of having to cook from scratch and make our own packed lunches was by simplifying our meals and being prepared. Last-minute shopping is almost impossible to achieve if you are aiming for zero plastic. We changed the way we stored food at home, using glass jars and beeswax wraps instead of Tupperware and cling film. I made a number of simple fabric drawstring bags to take to the shops, for buying fruit, veg, bread and other items, that we still use to this day. We started taking our own containers to the shops for cheese, fish and meat. Asking shop assistants to fill our containers rather than using a plastic bag was uncomfortable at first and quite often we were refused on grounds of hygiene or shop policies. But it always sparked a conversation with other shoppers and of course in the years since then, it has become a widely accepted practice. Because we were paying more attention, we noticed that several shops in our

'Everything we owned became more precious to us.'

area offered refills for olive oil, nuts and dried fruit, frozen fruit and even toiletries and cleaning products. In contrast to the anonymity of shopping at supermarkets, the experience of getting to know local shop owners and stallholders has been a heart-warming experience. People know us by name and are keen to help us shop plastic-free. We get to know how they run their businesses, how they procure their products and we know where our money goes.

After only three weeks we began to notice that we had very little rubbish and no plastic in our recycling bins. We were used to taking out the rubbish in big black plastic bags almost daily. Here we were with a huge bin with not much in it – indisputable physical evidence that something was working. There was no longer a dilemma whether, and how, different types of plastic and mixed materials could be recycled, whether our recycling was perhaps being shipped to poorer countries with little infrastructure to deal with it or whether it actually just ended up in landfill or an incinerator.

Much progress has been made in the last two years and independent zero-waste shops selling unpackaged foods and refills have sprung up all over the UK. In 2018, more than 40 companies that are responsible for over 80 per cent of plastic packaging on products sold through UK supermarkets joined the government, trade associations and campaigners to form the UK Plastics Pact. In 2019 a major supermarket retailer began trials of bulk dispensers and refill stations for unpackaged food, toiletries and cosmetics in a number of their stores. In 2020 there is much reason to feel hopeful and positive as single-use plastic bans continue to be implemented in many countries across the world.

We applied the principle of being prepared and simplifying to other areas of our household. We learned how to make toothpaste, deodorant and other simple toiletries to avoid plastic packaging, surprising ourselves with how easy it is and how effective they are. We switched to bamboo toothbrushes, soap bars, old-fashioned safety razors, and embarked on a search for the perfect shampoo soap bar. For cleaning the house we use vinegar, bicarbonate of soda and simple homemade products. We switched to cotton cloths, natural brushes and coconut fibre scrubbing pads. Laundry and washing up liquids can easily be refilled at local eco shops but we also experimented with soap nuts and other methods. Avoiding plastic packaging altogether and switching to more natural or homemade toiletries and cleaning products felt like a detox from chemicals and preservatives and the whole branded plastic bottle bonanza. Our home feels less cluttered and more natural.

There is something incredibly satisfying about learning how to make things that we previously

## Zero waste

Packaging-free shops selling loose goods have been popping up due to popular demand. Waitrose, Marks & Spencer and Asda have also trialled the idea. The initial trial, Waitrose Unpacked, in only a handful of outlets was overwhelmingly positive and extended to several further stores.

only ever bought in a shop. I experimented with growing sprouting seeds, watercress, basil and chillies in pots on the kitchen windowsill. It is a revelation how easy and cheap it is to make and grow things at home. A point in case was making windscreen wash for the car with just three ingredients costing literally a few pennies. There was a growing feeling of achievement and confidence in our ability to be self-reliant and resourceful. I am often asked whether it is more expensive to live the way we do. I think because there are so many items we refuse to buy in the first place and because we are prepared to repair items, buy secondhand and make things ourselves, we don't seem to spend more money than before.

We stopped buying online because this was the least successful method of avoiding plastic. Clothes and shoes were also extremely tricky with man-made fibres such as polyester dominating the fashion industry. This was an area where mending and secondhand shops came in handy. Everything we owned became more precious to us. The broken zip on an old backpack was replaced with a new one by a local seamstress, the loose sole of a pair of sheepskin slippers was sewn back on, old trousers were turned into shorts, worn-out clothes were made into fabric shopping bags and so on.

The year of the experiment presented us with many situations that required careful planning in order to avoid plastic: summer barbecues, Christmas celebrations, holidays, a big party for my husband's 50th, business travel and the daily challenges of work and school. We collected every bit of plastic packaging that we were unable to avoid during the first year, regardless of whether it could be recycled or not. We ended up with just one bagful of plastic waste.

A highlight of the year was being invited by our local Transition Town network organizers to give a public talk on living without plastic. The talk was so well attended that we offered a second one and formed a community action group under the umbrella of Transition Stroud. Our group, Stroud District Action on Plastic, has attracted funding from local benefactors to support a project coordinator and is engaged with individuals, civic institutions, community groups and businesses that are actively seeking to eliminate single-use plastic.

*Claudi Williams*

# claudi's practical tips + recipes

## Easy food hacks

There are some foods that are much easier and quicker to make than you might imagine and that can help you to avoid a ton of plastic like Tetra Pak cartons, tubs, bottles and bags. Some of the foods we make on a regular basis include hummus, coleslaw, marinated olives, patés, crackers, flat breads, muesli, granola, flapjacks, biscuits, jam, pickles, salad dressings and plant milks.

As a great alternative to dairy milk, plant milks have become a staple in many people's diets. If you are able to shop at a zero waste shop for unpackaged ingredients and have access to a blender, making your own plant milk couldn't be simpler. You need a piece of cheesecloth/muslin fabric to filter the pulp and a glass bottle to store the milk. Oat milk is one of the quickest and most sustainable plant milk recipes to make.

## Oat milk

Cover 100g of porridge oats with water and soak for 10 minutes. Drain the oats, add 750ml of fresh water and process in a blender until very smooth. For extra sweetness you could add a couple of pitted dates and a few drops of vanilla essence at the blending stage. Filter through a cheesecloth/ muslin and store in the fridge for up to five days. Use the leftover oat pulp to bake biscuits and to make granola.

The same method applies to other types of plant milks. Rice, hemp, nuts and seeds do have much longer soaking times. Cashews lend themselves to making an alternative to cream for use in Indian or vegan recipes. Simply soak a handful of cashews in a cup of water for 10 minutes and then blend – no need to strain afterwards.

## Storage and keeping food fresh

If you have Tupperware and cling film in your cupboards, do use those up, but consider these alternatives when buying new items:

- Glass jars and fabric bags for storing loose pasta, rice, lentils, muesli, nuts, seeds, herbs, flour and so on. You can use secondhand fabric to make the bags. If your jars are on display in your kitchen you might like to invest in some beautiful Kilner or Mason jars.

- Glass bottles for oil and vinegar refills.

- Tins for storing loose tea and coffee, biscuits and snacks.

- Beeswax or vegan food wraps to cover leftovers, wrap sandwiches and keep food fresh in and out of the fridge: bread, cheese, salad vegetables, fruit, fresh herbs and more. You can also use them in the freezer for up to a month.

- Lunch boxes that can double up as containers for buying unpackaged cheese, meat and fish. There are metal tiffin tins with clasps or bamboo boxes. Be warned though that some types of bamboo boxes and eco coffee cups for example contain toxic ingredients, glues and plastics such as formaldehyde and melamine.

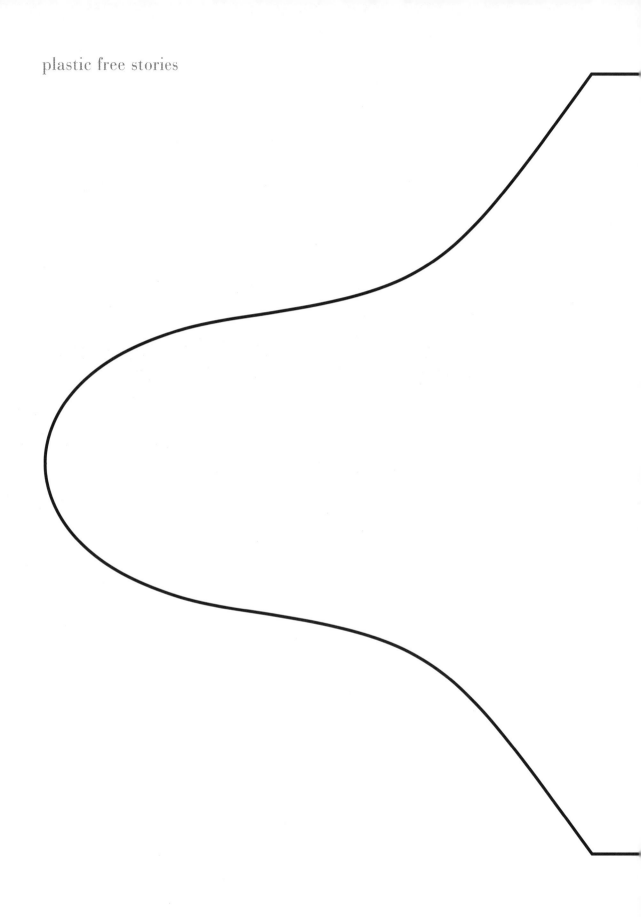

## Produce bag

Make your own produce bag for shopping and storing. You can make several in a variety of sizes for different uses, great for shopping at your local zero waste store. Use them for fruit, vegetables and all kinds of store-cupboard essentials such as lentils, flour or pasta.

- Use the template to cut out two shapes in washable fabric.
- Place right sides together and sew seams along the three straight sides.
- Neaten the raw edges with a zig-zag stitch.
- Turn the right way round and use the tops to tie the bag together.

### Template
Make several bags of different sizes to store different products. Weigh them first before weighing your produce.

## Basic cosmetics

Making cosmetics can be a complicated affair requiring many ingredients, which more often than not come in plastic containers. I resorted to a handful of simple recipes that are cheap and cheerful.

### Deodorant

This deodorant works well and is easy to apply with a folded cloth or flannel.

*2 heaped tbsp of Kaolin mineral clay*
*1 heaped tbsp of bicarbonate of soda (food grade)*
*a few drops of lavender essential oil or any other gentle essential oil*

- Simply mix the ingredients and store in a glass jar.

### Lip Balm

*10g of beeswax*
*3 tbsp of olive oil*
*3 tbsp of sunflower oil*
*a few drops of essential oils of your choice*

**How to make**

- Melt the wax and oil in a glass bowl over a pot with simmering water.
- Add a few drops of essential oil (mint, rose, geranium or lavender, for example).
- Pour into small tins or other small containers.

### Avocado, vanilla and lavender body butter

This lovely and deliciously scented cream for dry skin is also great as a hand cream or lip balm. A good online store for buying ingredients such as avocado butter is www.TheSoapKitchen.co.uk. I slightly adapted Wellness Mama's homemade natural lotion recipe as follows:

*half a cup grapeseed oil*
*quarter cup avocado butter*
*quarter cup beeswax*
*2 tbsp coconut oil*
*4 drops lavender essential oil*
*1 tsp vanilla extract*

**How to make**

- Melt all ingredients apart from the vanilla and lavender in a glass bowl over a pot with simmering water.
- Let the mixture cool a little and then add the vanilla and lavender.
- Pour into a glass jar or other container.
- Keeps well for several months.

## Toothpaste

Every year, billions of plastic toothpaste tubes and plastic toothbrushes are thrown away. I have read that every plastic toothbrush we have ever used still exists and will do so for hundreds of years. Toothpaste tubes are made with up to seven layers of different types of plastic and aluminum. Making your own toothpaste is simple and you don't need a degree in medicine. Talk to your dentist to find out what is and isn't good for your teeth and the best approach for children who might benefit from a fluoride toothpaste every now and then. There are many recipes and methods to be found in books and online. Some people swear by simple recipes such as three per cent peroxide and rosewater, or a little solid coconut oil and peppermint essential oil. Others recommend more complicated mixtures of herbal powders and essential oils beneficial to dental hygiene.

Below are my favourite three recipes, which I have adapted from various sources. Simply mix the ingredients together and store them in little glass jars. The toothpastes can easily be kept for a month or longer. My favourite recipe uses kaolin clay, a fine, white mineral clay that has a pleasant taste. If the peppermint is too strong for you, simply use less. Food-grade bicarbonate of soda has a low abrasion RDA (Relative Dentin Abrasion) value of 7. One very well-known brand for sensitive teeth has a value of 79 and some whitening brands hit the 150–250 mark, which is regarded as harmful.

### Kaolin clay toothpaste

This is a refreshing and at the same time gentle toothpaste.

*6 tbsp kaolin mineral clay*
*1 tbsp bicarbonate of soda (food grade)*
*5 tbsp vegetable glycerin*
*5 drops peppermint essential oil*
*5 drops sweet orange essential oil*

### How to make

- Mix the ingredients well and keep in a small glass jar for up to a month.
- Makes about 100ml, the same amount as an average tube of toothpaste.

### Coconut oil toothpaste

*1 tbsp coconut oil*
*1 tbsp bicarbonate of soda (food grade)*
*5–10 drops peppermint oil*
*2 drops lemon oil*
*2 drops orange oil*
*1 drop clove oil*

### How to make

- Mix the ingredients well and keep in a small glass jar.
- This makes a medium portion of toothpaste to last you for a few days.
- Use sparingly as the peppermint and clove oils are quite strong.
- Coconut oil tends to solidify when cold so your toothpaste may turn liquid on warm days and more solid on cold days.

I was able to source all the ingredients plastic-free by asking suppliers to help me out. The Kaolin clay is shipped in paper bags from abroad, or available in some zero waste shops.

Star Child of Glastonbury sell high quality essential oils in glass jars with metal lids. I buy the bicarbonate of soda in 2kg bags from a local bakery. Vegetable glycerin can be found in glass jars with metal lids in large Boots stores.

## Simple peppermint toothpaste

This recipe is for making a single portion at a time.

*1 tsp bicarbonate of soda (food grade)*

*1 tsp vegetable glycerin*

*3 drops peppermint essential oil*

### How to make

- Simply mix and use straightaway.

# Judit's story

## Toxic homes

ello, my name is Judit Németh-Rátfai, a forty-something mum of two based in Wotton-Under-Edge, Gloucestershire, with a passion for natural and sustainable living. I don't proclaim to be an expert, but I'm putting a lot of effort into trying to reduce our carbon footprint and dependence on single-use plastic and to provide a safe, natural home environment for my family.

I must admit, I have never been an enthusiastic cleaner and I think it goes back to my loathing of the harsh smell of shop-bought products. Like most of us, I kept using them in my home for years without thinking much about them, basically swimming in a toxic chemical soup.

My 'aha' moment came when my father was diagnosed with terminal cancer and passed away shortly after. He was a big advocate of using natural and traditional methods for cleaning and, as I become pregnant with my second child, I felt I really wanted to honour his legacy and protect my family, so I began a fast-paced shift towards greener living. Over the years this passion evolved into a hobby and a sort of side hustle of workshop hosting and talks on creating a homemade solution to cleaning. I love being part of the local community-led climate action network and really enjoy inspiring and helping people to make a switch towards a natural and sustainable lifestyle.

## Toxic homes

Manufactured cleaning products are harmful for us as well as the planet. According to numerous studies, the average household contains more than 60 environmental toxins that negatively affect our health. We're exposed to them routinely and it's been linked to many illnesses including asthma, cancer, autoimmune diseases, reproductive disorders, hormone disruption and neurotoxicity – just to name a few. Chronic exposure adds to the body's 'toxic burden' – the number of chemicals stored in its tissues at a given time. Furthermore, these products get into the water system, causing significant environmental harm and I haven't even started on the packaging...

## The homemade solution

The great news is that it's easy to minimize our exposure to these chemicals by making our own cleaning products that are much safer, 100 per cent natural and plant-based, very effective and a lot more cost-effective. With a relatively small amount of multipurpose natural supplies (significantly less compared to the arsenal of products available in shops), you can keep every area of your home, office and car clean and smelling amazing with the natural aromas of pure essential oils.

Many of these oils have great health and wellbeing benefits, such as supporting our immunity, so

## Five basic recipes

Please note, these recipes are made without using any preservatives, so they're safe to use for two to three weeks. It's better to make small amounts at a time and use them up within this timeframe. It's quick, easy and fun to mix up a solution when needed.

### Citrus bliss disinfectant spray

This bright disinfectant will leave your surfaces sparkly clean and your spaces smelling like summertime.

120ml glass bottle with spray cap

30ml rubbing alcohol

90ml water

20 drops lemon essential oil per bottle

15 drops bergamot essential oil per bottle

20 drops orange sweet essential oil per bottle

5 drops lime essential oil per bottle

**How to make**

- Fill the empty spray bottle with the water then add the rubbing alcohol.
- Add the essential oils one at a time, then put the cap on and shake gently prior to use.
- Note: you can use distilled vinegar instead of alcohol, and be wary of using this solution on polished wooden surfaces, you can also substitute the alcohol with a teaspoon of black soap – savon noir – a highly concentrated liquid made of 100% olive oil.

instead of surrounding yourself with harsh chemicals that can compromise your immunity and cause sensitivities as you clean, you can actually boost your and your family's health when you switch to natural cleaning. Are you ready to give it a go? For a starter, I have included five basic recipes here to try. Together we can change the world – one home at a time.

*Judit Németh-Rátfai*

### Fresh grout scrub-a-dub

Perfect for more stubborn stains/grease, cleaning for showers, tiles, countertops and sinks.

*500ml glass jar*
*1 cup bicarbonate of soda*
*3 tbsp castile soap*
*1 tbsp cornflour*
*1 tbsp white vinegar*
*10 drops tea tree essential oil*
*8 drops each of eucalyptus and peppermint essential oils*

**How to make**

- Add the bicarbonate of soda, cornflour, castile soap and vinegar to the jar and stir gently.
- Add the essential oils one at the time then put the cap on.
- Add more vinegar or castile soap as needed to make a smooth paste.
- Tip: if you have a mould problem in the bathroom, use 8 drops of palmarosa essential oil instead of eucalyptus – it has great antifungal properties.

### Natural sparkle glass cleaner

You can keep your windows, mirrors and other glass surfaces sparkly clean with this natural glass cleaner recipe. The essential oils of lavender and pink grapefruit not only leave a lovely, fresh and sweet aroma, they are also very effective at killing germs and bacteria – a win-win.

- *240ml glass bottle with a dispenser cap*
- *240 ml water*
- *2 tsp vinegar*
- *15 drops lavender essential oil*
- *15 drops pink grapefruit essential oil*

**How to make**

- Pour the water into the spray bottle then add the vinegar, followed by the essential oils.
- Give it a good shake before use.
- Tip: if you have newspapers at home, they make a great glass cleaner.

### Limescale buster spray

If you, like us, have a constant battle with limescale in your house, this recipe is a revelation. Citric acid is a well-known limescale buster, so use it generously on the toilet, taps and shower screens.

*500ml glass bottle with a dispenser cap*
*500 ml water*
*2 tbsp citric acid*
*10 drops lemon essential oil*
*5 drops lime essential oil*

**How to make**

- In a measuring jug, mix the water and citric acid then pour the solution into the spray bottle.
- Add the essential oils.
- Give it a good shake before use.
- Tip: this solution is also great for dealing with stubborn fruit stains.

### Bucketful solution for clean floors

Simple yet so effective. Just mix it up in a minute then wipe your floors clean.

*Bucket and floor wipe/mop*
*3–4 litres warm water*
*2 tbsp black soap*
*5 drops lemon essential oil*
*5 drops lavender essential oil*

**How to make**

- Add the water to the bucket, followed by the black soap and essential oils.

## What's in my cupboard?
## The cleaning essentials

- bicarbonate of soda – cleans, deodorises, softens water, scours
- white vinegar – dissolves dirt, grease, grime and kills bacteria naturally
- basic washing soap, plant-based (I grate it down to make my washing powder)
- Castile soap – 100% plant-based, natural and pure liquid made of vegetable oils – very safe for sensitive skin
- liquid black soap (savon noir with olive oil) – highly concentrated, most amazing multi-purpose cleaner that's 100% natural and very effective
- citric acid – brilliant for limescale
- washing soda (sodium carbonate) – more caustic than bicarbonate of soda, cuts grease, removes wax and lipstick
- rubbing alcohol – when you need more cleaning power (oven, sink, taps)
- borax substitute – water softener, disinfectant and deodoriser
- essential oils – those with antiviral, antibacterial, antimicrobial and antifungal properties are recommended, including citrus oils such as lemon, lime, orange, mandarin, pink grapefruit, bergamot, peppermint, eucalyptus, tea tree, lavender, Siberian fir, ravintsara and palmarosa

# judit's top hacks around the house

- I don't know about you, but I'm pretty worried about bacteria proliferating on my washing up loofah sponges, bamboo wipes and brushes. Luckily, it's really easy to keep them fresh and germ-free. You can just add a couple of drops of undiluted lemon essential oil to the surface and leave it overnight or make a small bottle of sponge-cleaner spray: fill a 30ml bottle with a spray cap with water then add 18 drops of lemon essential oil to it. Always give it a vigorous shake before use and make a fresh bottle every three to four weeks. This hack is also great for keeping your chopping boards clean.

- For a fresh-smelling bathroom, keep a bunch of eucalyptus by the shower. The steam releases the aroma and essential oils from the leaves, so you feel like you're in a spa.

- Natural hand cleanser on the go – great for adults and kids, it's gentle and effective, reducing microbial activity wherever you go. Fill a small, 60ml bottle (ideally with pop-up caps) with aloe vera gel and add 4 drops of pink grapefruit oil, 4 drops of lavender oil and 4 drops of Siberian fir.

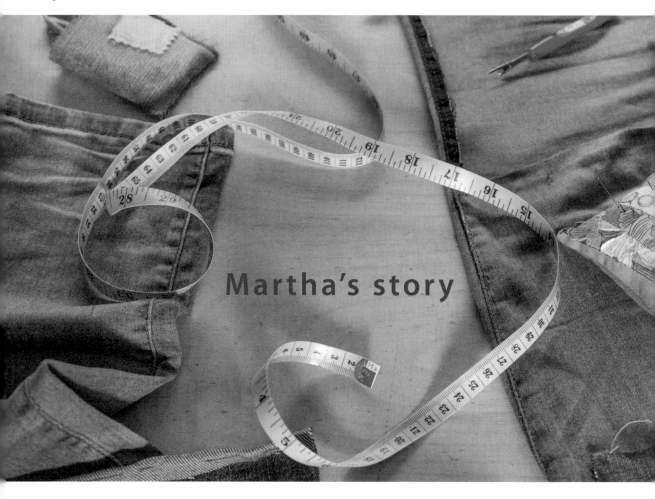

Martha's story

## The Sewing Shed

In the early 2000s I made bespoke garments from my studio in Bristol. I loved it and built up a longstanding customer base. Then one day a new client asked me to design and make a dress for her. I gave her a quote and she was utterly shocked with the given price and told me, 'I can buy that much cheaper in a shop.' I replied, 'That is true, but I can't live on £1 an hour!'

This brought home to me that the cheap clothes produced for the Western market mean that the skills used to create them are no longer valued, resulting in worldwide exploitation. All so we can wear cheap clothes, have a big choice and not pay the real price for it.

Then in 2013, the inevitable happened, the collapse of a neglected and overcrowded building, the eight-storey commercial property called Rana Plaza, in Dhaka, Bangladesh, which made clothes for popular Western brands. More than 1,000 people died. It is often women and children who do these poorly paid jobs and they don't have the opportunity or education to get out of their situation. This exploitation of people, the total disrespect for materials and our throwaway culture made me change my shopping habits for myself and my family.

It is better to make clothes ourselves and to teach others to do the same, as it not only develops an appreciation of the skills needed for the creation

process but it also has a huge feel-good effect. The sense of achievement and huge satisfaction I see on people's faces gives me a buzz. I run regular workshops and courses at The Sewing Shed, Stroud, teaching people the basics of dressmaking and passing on my skills, so they have the wherewithal to 'do it themselves'. The process of making is not only good for the planet, as you will really want to look after a homemade piece of clothing, but you can also keep altering it, restyling it and keep on wearing it.

*Martha van der Laan*
sewingshedstroud.co.uk

# martha's projects

**Mend your jeans**

**1+1 makes a new top**

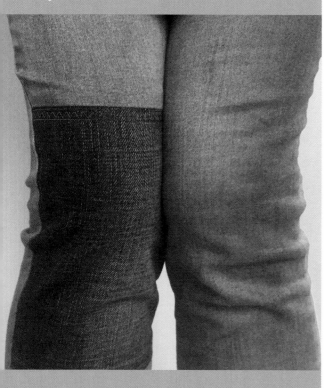

## Mend your jeans

Hole on your knee? Add a big patch and re-style your favourite jeans for a few more years of wear.

*Your old jeans*
*A patch of denim or other fabric from another garment*
*Scissors*
*Pencil or tailors' chalk*
*Sewing machine*
*Thread*

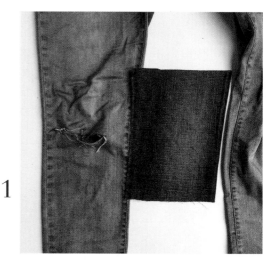

**1**

- Draw lines across your trouser leg to mark where you want to add your new piece of fabric.
- Cut a big enough patch to cover the whole width of your trousers adding a 1.5cm (½in) seam allowance on all four sides.
- Press and neaten all raw edges with a zigzag stitch or overlocker.

**2**

- Unpick both side seams, plus an extra 10cm (4in) on each corner to create access.
- Cut across your trouser leg from seam to seam following your drawn line, press and neaten the edges.
- Pin your new piece of fabric onto your trouser leg right sides facing, stitch leaving approximately 1.5cm (½in) seam allowance and press seams.

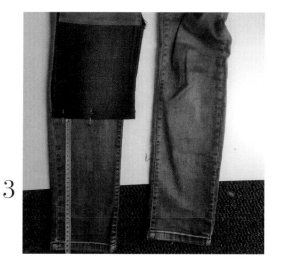

3

- If you would like to add a decorative stitch this is the time to do it.
- Repeat on the other side so that both seams across the leg are closed.
- Make sure your second seam is straight by measuring the distance from the ground along your seam.

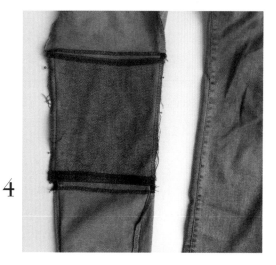

4

- Turn your trousers inside out and pin both side-seams so that the seams are exactly lined up.
- Try and stitch in the existing seam in your trouser leg so that the new panel fits in smoothly.
- Stitch, neaten and press both seams.

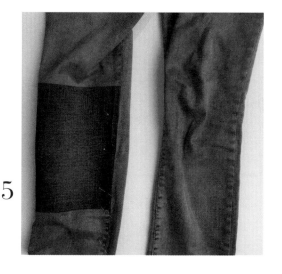

5

- Turn your trousers right side out.
- You only need to finish the seam on the inside leg. Press this seam, which is inside your trousers, towards the front of the trousers. This is the same direction the seam was pressed towards before you unpicked the side seam.
- Pin all the three layers and top stitch the inside seam to the front trouser leg to secure the seam.

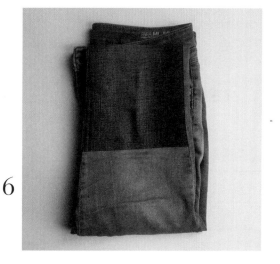

6

- Make sure you match the colour of your stitches to the existing thread and voilà, your favourite trousers are ready to be worn again.

## 1+1 makes a new top

This project transforms a skirt and a cardigan that are past their useful lives into a whole new top with a turtle neck that you will want to wear.

*A long-sleeved, woollen, knitted cardigan*
*A stretch-cotton jersey skirt with a wide waistband*
*Light- to medium-weight fusible interfacing*
*Wadding (optional)*
*Sewing machine*
*Thread*

**Sleeves:**

* Start by marking your left and right sleeves and also marking what is front and back of each cardigan sleeve before cutting them off and using them as your pattern.

* Place your left sleeve against your right sleeve, touching in the middle, to get one whole sleeve pattern.
* Pin the pattern on a double layer of fabric.
  Adding approximately 1.5cm (½in) for a seam allowance along the top and sides, cut out two sleeves.

* Fold right sides together, pin and sew the side seams of your sleeves and neaten the edges.

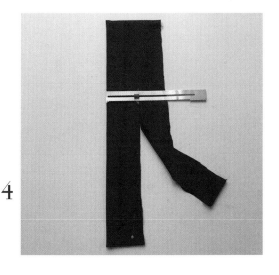

4

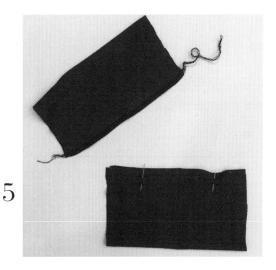
5

### Cuffs:

- Cut two cuffs from the waistband of your skirt. They should be double the end width of your sleeve and twice the depth required.
- Save the rest of the waistband for the front panel.

- Fold the cuffs right sides together, sew the long edge first, and then turn them right side out, with the finished edge inside.
- Sew the short sides together and neaten the seam.

6

7

- Pin the cuffs inside your sleeve, right side of cuff to right side of sleeve, sew around the edge and neaten the seam with a zigzag stitch or overlocker.

- Pin the right side of the sleeve into the right side of the sleeve hole.
- Stitch around the sleeve hole and neaten the rough edges with a zigzag stitch or overlocker.

8

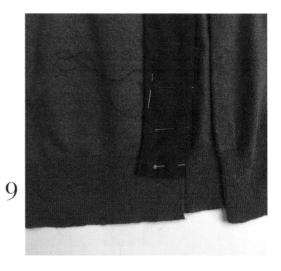

9

**Front panel piece:**

- Fold right sides together, sew the short edges and turn right side out and press.
- Cut front panel piece to your preferred width.
- Unpick the button stand and remove the buttons. To reinforce, attach light- to medium-weight fusible interfacing on the inside where you will attach the front panel.

- Position the panel by lining up the rough edges with the centre front seam.
- Pin the panel in place making sure it is completely flat. Sew the panel by hand using small stitches and regular sewing thread.

10

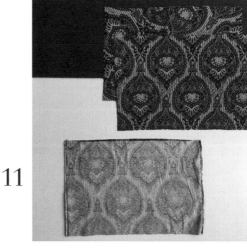

11

- Fold the centre edge of the right side under by 1cm (⅜in) to create a neat edge.
- Place right side approximately 1cm (⅜in) over the left side and pin in place, starting at the top and bottom and working your way inwards to make sure the top and bottom are lined up.
- Use embroidery thread and a blanket stitch or running stitch to attach both front panels.

**Cowl neck:**

- Using a tape measure standing on its side, measure the neckline, starting at the centre back, about 64cm (25in). Decide the height of your collar, about 20cm (7½in), and cut two rectangular pieces of fabric about 64cm × 20cm (25in × 7½in).
- With right sides together, sew the short edges on both panels. You will now have two loops of fabric.

12

- Put one inside the other, right sides facing and wrong sides out, pin and stitch along the top edge.
- Turn your collar right side out, folding in half with wrong sides facing each other and press the fold.
- Pin the raw edges together and finish this edge of your collar.

13

- If your collar needs more volume and is too floppy you can add wadding.
- Cut out your stiffener in the same shape as your collar and sew into a cylinder shape and add it to the inside of your collar.
- Attach this to the seam allowance of your actual collar.

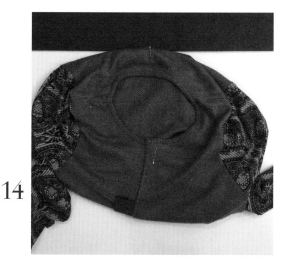

14

- Divide your bodice neckline into four equal parts and mark with pins.
- Repeat the same process on your collar.
- Pin both raw edges of the collar to the right side of the bodice neckline, aligning the four pins on the collar and neckline.

15

- Make sure that the seams on your collar end up on the inside.
- Stitch the collar to the bodice neckline.
- The neckline might need to stretch so don't use too short a stitch; 2½–3mm (³⁄₃₂ – ⅛in) long should work well.
- Press your new garment well and enjoy your newly made top.

# Peter's story

I experienced a tipping point shortly after Claudi and I started to eradicate disposable plastic from our household as she describes earlier in this book. Learning how easy it was to make three simple items in particular – toothpaste, deodorant and household cleaner – gave me the impression that we suffer from a collective shortsightedness when it comes to personal accountability. It demonstrated to me just how much we can do as individuals to repair our planet.

The level of debate around plastic and its alternatives currently seems predicated on unaltered or slightly altered lifestyles. It falls short of challenging the huge over-consumption that we collectively drive. Consideration is rarely given to a full re-evaluation of what we think we 'deserve' as 'consumers'. For example, we listen to debates about the unintended consequences of replacing plastic bags with paper ones whilst the opportunity exists to repurpose fabric and, with a little discipline, use fabric bags to ensure we never use either plastic OR paper. Replacing plastics in the supply chain is commented on by eminent scientists and economists but mostly without consideration being given to whether supply chains are responsible.

Our decision to make our own toothpaste, deodorant and household cleaner, amongst other things, means that I walk through shop aisles that are now irrelevant. Having 'banked' the fact that our homemade alternatives seemed to be better, simpler, cheaper and environmentally positive, my mind wanders to the incredible scale of the businesses that sell the consumer choice and myth of convenience that I once contributed to. For a while back in the 1990s I recruited marketers for Fast Moving Consumer Goods companies. Great minds were put to work in category management – the art and science of helping the consumer believe that they needed the latest variation of the right formula and be able to pick it up wherever they need it. There was a pathological pursuit of volume; margin and the SKU (stock keeping unit) all bound up in the relentless pursuit of competitive advantage, brand dominance and profit. Just as it was not in the interests of the oil lobby to let electric vehicles emerge as an alternative to the internal combustion engine in the 40s, there is not a lot of representation or lobbying for the benefits of a bar of soap, a bit of vinegar and bicarbonate of soda being sufficient for all of our home cleaning needs (they are!).

A few years of living without plastic prompted me to reflect. I consider that we have been part of a mass 'sleep walk' into the consumerist myth started in the postwar years. The subsequent cynicism and anti-competitive practices shown by many consumer businesses has built an infrastructure that is only slowly being challenged. I also recruited for Coca Cola Schweppes

> ❝I consider that we have been part of a mass "sleep walk" into the consumerist myth started in the postwar years.❞

Beverages as they launched their mission to, effectively, compete with water, which resulted in their products displacing water in parts of the world that can least afford it in terms of both money and health. Looking in detail at the infrastructure and its consequences has led us as a family to address the habitual consumption that underlies the state of the world as we slowly wake up from the binge.

I suppose there must be a madly idealistic streak in me to expect a mass adoption of home making cleaning products so that, overnight, we can all give up the acres of brightly coloured bottles and packets (and the insulting TV adverts that go with them) and move on to the next improvement. I now have to admit to standing in shops watching in disbelief as people load up with Cif, Jif, Cillit Bang and other pollutants.

I can't claim to be a 'postmaterialist' and there are plenty of ways in which our carbon footprint could be improved but the current phase of consumption reduction sees us enjoying the thrift of buying secondhand, making do and mending, as well as refurbishment. As we make new decisions and new habits based on seasonal availability, manufacturing process, supply chain implications and food miles etc., it reinforces how much we had previously regarded availability and choice as our right.

I'd like to think that we have an ethical and noble motivation that drives us and to some degree I think we do. However, it is knowing that I will never again give a penny to companies that package for profit that helps me through the dark times of denying myself a piece of tasteless fruit or veg from the other side of the world or removing limescale by hand and citric acid rather than with a 'magic formula'. Now that we've started, I feel a zeal for seeing it through and showing ourselves and anyone else who might be interested that the effort to change habits is worth it. Our purchase is a vote and we can collectively move from consumer to citizen in a way that will support the social enterprise and ethically anchored organisations we need in order to meet the needs of the planet and its inhabitants. It is happening now and the new zeitgeist is moving fast. I have faith that the response from the business world will increasingly improve as the enlightened customer asks the questions and makes new choices based on individual, social and environmental accountability. There is a big difference, and an important psychological step, between deciding to do something and actually doing it: turning a sense of accountability into action. On that psychological pivot rests the opportunity to protect the future.

To end on a practical note, below are some ideas for a less wasteful way of tackling DIY – an area of our household that falls mainly to me. Using some of these options, I have built a porch almost entirely from materials from an old conservatory, an outside decking area, a shed, cupboards in the utility room and the attic and refurbished our kitchen, including the wooden floors.

*Peter Williams*

### Aggregate

If you need sand, gravel, top soil etc., you can buy loose from a building supplier and have it delivered or pick it up with a truck or large car. We have bought even small amounts by taking our metal buckets along to a local building merchant.

### Cable ties

Consider alternatives – depending on the job you may be able to use wire, rope, string etc.

### Carpets

All carpets have a polymer underlay or underside. See if you can choose a wooden floor instead or, if it has to be carpet, make sure it's woollen, coir, sisal, seagrass or jute.

### Cement mix

Choose cement mix in paper sacks.

### Curtains and blinds

Consider buying secondhand; choose a natural fabric and wooden/metal poles and rings. If you're buying blinds watch out for 'faux wood' and plastic fittings – there are non-plastic versions available that are not much more expensive.

### Dust sheets

Ditch the plastic tarpaulin and poly dust sheets and use old bed sheets instead.

### Floor insulation

Look for modern eco-friendly insulation such as wool fleece, for example. Use specialist wooden slithers to fill floor board gaps.

### Gloves

Use fabric and leather gloves for heavy work. Use biodegradable latex gloves for paint and varnish work if needed.

### Glue

You can get most types of glue in tins rather than plastic tubs or tubes.

### Guttering

Choose metal guttering – again, look for used items first.

### Lamps

For lamps choose wood, copper, pewter, fabric or glass, new or secondhand. Choose brass and copper bulb holders, fabric flexes instead of electrical plastic cables and wood and brass ceiling roses.

### Paintbrushes and rollers

Choose brushes and roller holders with wooden handles. There are biodegradable rollers made from recycled materials on the market. Wash out rollers and paint brushes and look after them well to give them a long life.

### Paint

Choose eco-paints free from acrylic, oil and vinyl in metal tins from natural ranges such as Auro, Earthborne or Little Greene. Avoid plastic paint buckets and plastic handles on paint pots.

### Pavingstones, mantles, doors, fireplace, floorboards and flagstones

Find an architectural salvage yard or other local supplier, try antiques shops, or check on Freecycle, Gumtree and eBay. If you can pick it up locally and it is pre-used, it will almost certainly be packaging free.

### Plumbing fittings

Look for secondhand sinks, bathtubs, loos etc. If buying new, choose ceramic over plastic, get a bamboo loo seat with stainless steel fittings, which last much longer. Choose copper pipes and metal fittings over plastic ones generally.

### Multipurpose filler

Choose a filler mix in cardboard boxes without an extra plastic bag inside.

### Power sockets

Choose metal power sockets fittings and plates.

### Rope

Instead of plastic rope, consider traditional hemp rope, which many DIY shops sell on reels by the metre.

### Screws and nails

Find a shop that sells these loose or in cardboard boxes – often much cheaper too. Save odd screws and nails for the next DIY job. Recycle old screws and nails at your local household recycling centre. There are wooden rawlplugs available on the internet.

### Silicone and caulk

Choose silicone guns made entirely form metal. Some caulk refill bottles come in cardboard instead of plastic.

### Tools

Choose wooden-handled tools – buy secondhand if possible. Flea markets are superb for finding well-made tools and you can also try Gumtree and Freecycle groups online. Share your power tools with others. Borrow the power tools you need from friends and family. Some towns have tool libraries.

### Varnish

Consider natural oils instead of varnish. Buy varnish in glass jars or tins instead of plastic bottles.

### White spirit

Buy large metal tins instead of plastic bottles. White spirit does not go off.

### Windows

Use aluminium or wooden windows. There are huge amounts of secondhand windows available with perfectly good glass.

### Wood

Reuse any wood that you or your friends might be getting rid of. Find out where your local saw mill or local wood supplier is and get a personalised service. If you need doors or windows you might find something at the salvage yard, on Freecycle or from a local supplier.

# Katy's story

## A Crafter's contribution

We're lucky enough to live outside a town and to have a large garden, so we compost everything and use the lovely organic matter created on the flower and vegetable beds. Last year I found myself picking out small squares of plastic from the wheelbarrow, finally working out that these are the paper bags that our teabags are sealed in. I wrote to the company which insisted that these need to be plastic lined to keep the tea fresh, but I decided to stop using teabags altogether, digging out our teapot and reinstating the tea-strainer and the cosy. I like a cup of herbal tea and realised that we have plenty of these plants in the garden, from nettles to lemon balm, growing quite wildly. Since then I have tried planting things to use for teas as well, such as fennel and sage. The camomile was less successful, when I planted a crop of dyer's camomile rather than the kind used for calming infusions.

I am keen on recycling, our great achievement measured by the quantity of recycling we were able to produce especially since we eventually produced more recycling than 'black bin' waste. Then I was horrified to read some statistics about how much recycling ends up not being reused, either because it hasn't been washed, has been put in the wrong bin, or just for lack of recycling facilities ends up in landfill anyway and realised that just recycling everything isn't the answer.

Now we get our milk in refillable bottles and the amount of plastic we are throwing away has halved. We buy packaging-free when we can, but

"We have to believe that the small things we do, especially if they catch on, can make a difference."

40

these options are often only available if you live in the right place or have the money to pay for them. However, there are small things that we can do in our own ways. I'm not ready for a vegan diet, but we eat less meat than we used to and are conscientious about using up and freezing food with the minimum of waste. My mother, brought up during the war, had all these economies drilled into her and so it was at home. Food cooked one day became the stock for a soup or stew and the leftovers were meals for days to come. These skills seem to be lost to a new generation, more used to heating up ready meals in black plastic pots and throwing away perfectly good food past the date on its packaging.

Recognising the value of things is important, not just so that we treat things with respect but so that we look after them too. When you realise that some things are irreplaceable it is worth mending and repairing them. These things may have

sentimental value or are just so useful that you don't want to lose them.

The current model of our economy is based upon the concept that progress is reliant on continuous growth. That means we are encouraged to keep using, keep buying and keep throwing away. With reduced resources this is not a sustainable option. Apart from the occasional election and campaigning it can feel like there is nothing we can do, but there is. The cultural anthropologist Margaret Mead said, 'Never doubt that a small group of thoughtful committed citizens can change the world; indeed, it's the only thing that ever has.' We have to believe that the small things we do, especially if they catch on, can make a difference.

*Katy Bevan*
@thecrafter_uk

## Make-up remover pad

If you wear make-up the chances are you also use cotton wool to remove it. These little pads mean you won't have to throw anything away, just pop them in a washing bag and clean with the rest of your laundry. I made these with double knitting yarn and a medium-sized hook, but you can use whatever you have in your stash, as long as it is soft and washable. Dishcloth cotton is ideal.

*DK cotton yarn*
*4mm (US G/6) crochet hook*
Abbreviations: ss=slip stitch; ch=chain; dc=double crochet (US sc); st=stitch; rep=repeat

### How to make

Start with a magic ring, or 3ch and ss into first ch to make a ring, 6dc in ring.

- 1st round: 2dc in each st.
- 2nd round: 1dc, 2dc in next st, rep to end.
- 3rd round: 1dc in next 2 sts, 2dc in next st, rep to end.
- 4th round: 1dc in next 3 sts, 2dc in next st, rep to end.
- 5th round: 1dc in next 4sts, 2dc in next st, rep to end.
- Fasten off and weave in end.

### Flannel:

To make a flannel, make a chain the width that you want it to be, say 20cm (8in) and work double crochet or half treble crochet stitches, with a 1 or 2ch standing chain at the start of each row.

- Work back and forth until you have a square.
- Fasten off and sew in the ends.
- Neaten the edges with a border around if you wish.

## Make your own yarn

The yarn arts are a marvellous thing, but unless you have your own flock of sheep, materials can be expensive and hard to source sustainably. The answer is to reuse any clothes that are too worn out to go to a charity shop. Here I have a favourite old jumper which had already been mended many times in an attempt to extend its life. Stretchy jersey and T-shirt materials are best to use and woollens that won't fray or unravel. It is also possible to buy T-shirt yarn that is a by-product of the fashion industry, perfect for making rugs, bathmats or larger items.

The width of your strips will be dictated in part by the fabric you are cutting. Finer fabric will lend itself to thinner strips and then you can use a smaller crochet hook or knitting needles. For wider strips and quick projects you can find crochet hooks up to 25mm diameter (US 50).

**1**

- Lay out your garment and cut off the main body below the sleeves.

**2**

- Cut off the sleeves.

**3**

- Fold the body over several times towards one of the folded edges. Make incisions 1–2cm (⅜in) apart, being careful not to cut through the folded edge.

**4**

- Do the same with the sleeve, though you may not have to fold it up.

**5**

- Starting at one edge, clip diagonally across the fold from one strip to the next.

**6**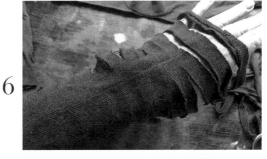

- It may be easier to put your arm in the middle so you can see what you are doing.

**7**

- To use the rest of your garment, lay it out flat and cut across, nearly to the edge and then back to create a continuous strip.

**8**

- Roll your strips up into balls and repeat the process with other garments.

# Lavoni's story

I remember clearly the night I watched the documentary *Plastic China* (2016, directed by Jiuliang Wang). I woke up at 2am concerned about the children who grew up in the plastic recycling factories – they could be my children – since then I have been very aware of every single purchase, especially those which contain plastic or any other single-use object.

In the culture that I grew up in we were naturally pretty much zero waste. I still use the metal lunch box that every child would take to school each day. As time went on though, disposable goods became more and more prevalent. Growing up, I was concerned with waste and pollution and this sentiment has only grown stronger as the waste and disposable culture has accelerated to alarming levels.

Becoming a mother over a decade ago was an important point in my life, as we tend to reflect more deeply about what kind of Earth and society we want our children to inherit as well as providing a role model for them in the way we live and conduct ourselves. I also started to make my own sanitary pads, as I was keen to stop using any kind of disposable hygiene products. After more

than ten years of using my own pads I have refined and improved them, proving that they really are a great green alternative.

At this time I also came into contact with the teachings of P.R. Sarkar, which have inspired me in many ways, including my ecological outlook. He advises that we need a moral base before we can develop internally, so as to develop mental equipoise or balance, so that we can develop ourselves as humans. Two parts of this moral base, of which there are ten main points, are *aparigraha* and the other is *ahimsa*, both Sanskrit terms. *Aparigraha* means to not take anything which is superfluous to your life. This can change over time and alter from culture to culture. In terms of zero waste this is particularly pertinent, as we are often implicitly taught that we can greedily consume products without overly worrying about the consequences, as there are appropriate bins for all the waste to be put in to be recycled. However, people are now waking up to the problems and complications associated with recycling, that although it is good to recycle our waste, it still consumes energy and creates pollution to do so. So I feel that taking this concept of *aparigraha* into our lives and asking ourselves whether we really

need something, whether it is a new cooking pot, a flight to Barcelona or a second car will make a difference. The other concept *ahimsa*, means non-violence. We can extend this to other creatures and inanimate objects, such as our environment. This also led to me becoming vegan. A few years ago I became aware of a statistic, that if the whole world was to become vegan then we could do away with 70 per cent of agricultural land. Although unrealistic at present, I feel this is a direction human society should be moving in.

A few years ago, although I was doing these things to reduce waste, I was still buying disposable packing, especially food on products. Then, after seeing the *Plastic China* documentary, I decided I would really commit to not using disposable plastic anymore.

For me the zero-waste journey is not something to be compartmentalised, but to be considered as part of an overall holistic life attitude. It's not a competition about who can use the least plastic. It concerns our relationship with our community and our ability to solve our collective problems. I see it as part of a subtler practise of ridding ourselves of not only physical waste but also mental waste, which we can all too easily collect in life.

*Lavoni Norman*
@maximum_utilization

‘It's not a competition about who can use the least plastic. It concerns our relationship with our community and our ability to solve our collective problems.’

## Sanitary pads

There are as many ways to make sanitary pads as you can imagine, and the best way is the one that works for you.

The smallest template included in the book is for discharge or very light flow, for this you only need one thin layer of filler. The medium-sized one is for regular flow; you need two to four fillers, depending on your personal need. The big one is for nighttime use; I made it particularly long to avoid the chance of sheets getting stained. This one can be as thick as a nappy, because you usually don't move a lot at night. But if you like the security of the length and want to wear it during the day, two to three fillers inside is also fine. It's an art to make it thick enough to hold the blood while being mobile and feeling free. There's no perfect answer to fit everyone's needs as our flows are all different. I also want to emphasise that you can always adjust the template – make it a little shorter or longer, add bigger wings or copy your favourite disposable pads by tracing around them for your template.

*Snap fasteners*
*Layers of washed cotton fabrics*
*Thread*
*Sewing machine or needle*

**How to make**

- Using the template, cut out two pieces of cotton fabric of your choice – they will be the top and bottom pieces.
- Cut three fillers from the template. They can be different fabrics, for example a layer of T-shirt material, a layer of towel and a layer of waterproof material.
- Pin the fillers on the wrong side of the top piece and sew them together.
- Sew the top and bottom piece together, wrong sides facing outwards. Remember to leave a gap.
- Turn the filler inside out through the gap and sew around the edges.
- Sew the snap fasteners on.
- Before using your pads for the first time, wash them in the washing machine, or by hand, allowing for approximately five per cent shrinkage.
- If using new materials, wash your fabric before you make the pads; recycled fabrics shouldn't have this shrinkage problem.

**Washing**

- Soak the used pad in cold tap water as soon as you can for 10 minutes (hot water makes fresh blood congeal).
- Rinse and rub some soap on, soak for another 10 minutes.
- Rinse and if it's still dirty, repeat step 2 until it's clean.
- For extra cleaning, put it in the washing machine.
- Try hydrogen peroxide or bicarbonate of soda to remove stains and odours.

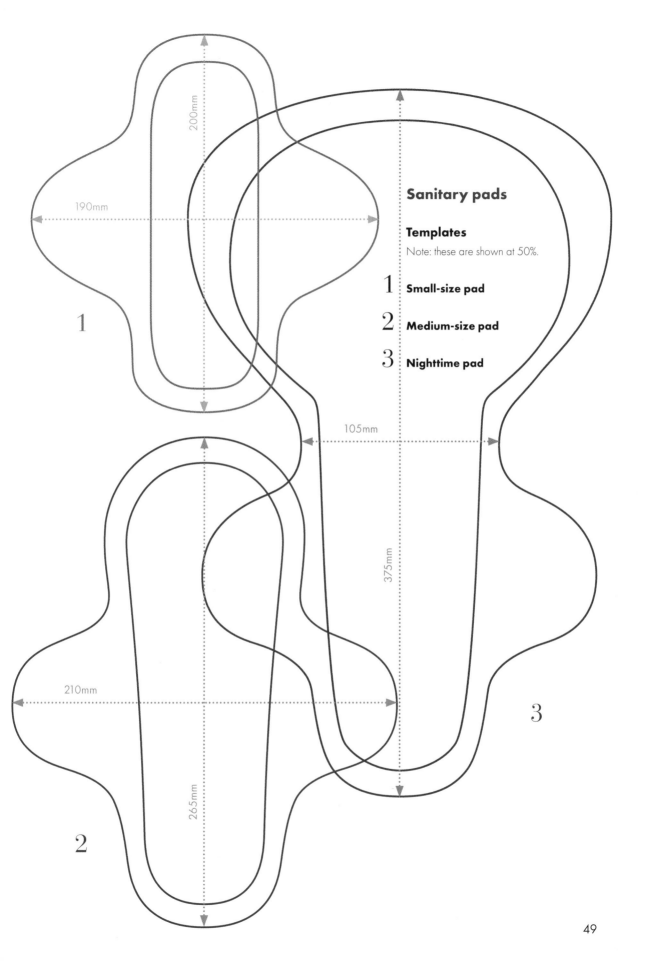

**Sanitary pads**

**Templates**
Note: these are shown at 50%.

1 **Small-size pad**

2 **Medium-size pad**

3 **Nighttime pad**

1

2

3

200mm

190mm

105mm

375mm

210mm

265mm

# Carly's story

I grew up in a small town in Central British Columbia, Canada, called Williams Lake, a heavily meat-eating, rural community. However, I have never eaten meat. I didn't know of any other vegetarians and there were no food alternatives, and no vegetarian options at any restaurants.

On the flip side, our milk came in glass bottles, groceries were packed in paper bags and my mom only used reusable nappies. We were also fortunate to have a garden. When my mom would pack our lunch for school she would head to the garden to get all the essentials: fresh carrots, radishes, lettuce and anything else that she could use. We also had access to different fruits in our yard, such as crab apples, raspberries, gooseberries, strawberries and blackcurrants. To get our family through the harsh winters, my Dad made a cold cellar under the garden where he would store different vegetables to keep them fresh. A Williams Lake winter means around five months of snow in -10°C to -40°C temperatures.

These 'eco-friendly' measures were not done necessarily to benefit the environment, instead they were done to save money or because that was the only thing available at that time. To think that so much has changed in just thirty years is scary. Climate change became news around 30 years ago, yet since then we have experienced excessive consumerism and increased plastic use.

When I moved to the UK in 2015, I began to reflect on the amount of plastic waste that we generate. I wanted to make changes in areas that I could control, one of which was the simple change of eliminating our use of cling film. My husband and I started experimenting with making our own beeswax wraps. After a lot of research and prototyping we ended up with a really great product that we thought everyone should have. I went on to create a company that manufactured beeswax wraps with a friend from Bristol and three years later we had saved hundreds of thousands of metres of clingfilm from ending up in landfill. I am no longer associated with that company but the product continues to greatly reduce the use of cling film.

In the midst of starting a new and rapidly growing business, our little girl, Florence, was born in March 2018 and she is quite literally the best baby in the world (biased, me?). As amazing as motherhood is, I feel that having a baby is the biggest personal challenge on my plastic-free journey so far. Modern life is heavily geared towards single-use plastics in baby products. I know as a working mom I have had more than a few weak moments of not being organised enough to make all of Flo's food from scratch, or I haven't had enough time to wash all the reusable nappies in time to reuse them. I am not by any means an expert on being a plastic-free mom, but I have learnt many good tips and recipes along the way

> ‘If you use one reusable nappy once a day you could save up to 365 disposable nappies going into land fill every year.’

that I hope will inspire some of you to make those changes with your family.

## Tackling the nappy mountain

An estimated three billion disposable nappies are used every year in the UK. That is a crazy amount, especially when most disposable nappies don't get recycled and end up in landfill or get burnt. Throwaway nappies not only contain plastic but are packaged in it as well. According to Friends of the Earth, they can take up to 500 years to break down, and even when they do they will produce methane which contributes to global warming. In the long run reusable nappies will save you money. It is said that by the time children are potty trained they will have used up to 6,000 disposable nappies, which will go directly into landfill. To save on water, I do also suggest that when you clean your reusable nappies you wait until you have a full load of washing.

There is some good news too: disposable nappies create so much household waste that the UK Government has now started taking action on this. There are plans to set up a Government-led campaign to promote reusable nappies and help families cut down on single-use plastic, which is a huge step. The Nappies (Environmental Standards) Bill 2017–19, will encourage all local authorities to implement the scheme that will help people to start using reusable nappies. I feel extremely lucky that

Gloucester has a scheme already in place to help parents purchase reusable nappies. I took advantage of this and bought from the company Tot Bots. Stroud Maternity Hospital also provides you with a reusable nappy when you have a baby there.

It's not always easy or practical to make the change. It took me a while to start taking full advantage of reusable nappies. Even if you use one reusable nappy once a day you could save up to 365 disposable nappies going into landfill every year.

### Nappy rash

- The UK disposes of around 3 billion disposable nappies each year, representing an estimated 2% to 3% of all household waste.
- By the time one baby is potty trained the baby could use 4,000 to 6,000 disposable nappies. In comparison, a baby only needs around 20 to 30 modern reuseable nappies and these can also be used by any siblings that come along.
- Although reuseable nappies cost a few pounds each initially and need to be laundered, they can save parents around £200 to £500 over 2.5 years for their first baby and even more if reused for subsequent children. Source: wrap.org.uk

## Baby wipes

The next difficulty is baby wipes, most of which are full of plastic polymers and harmful chemicals such as detergents, moisturisers, fragrances and preservatives. You have to do some research to find ones that are bio-degradable, plastic free and don't contain nasty chemicals. The best thing to do is just have some damp cotton cloths in a wet bag to bring with you when you go out. If you are in the comfort of your own home it is easy enough to wet the cloth and use that. Cotton cloths are not only handy for using as reusable wipes, but they can also work well when cleaning your baby once it starts eating. After Flo eats we only use one cotton cloth to clean her, her table and the floor, in that order. It is a great tip to take up. The cloth gets rinsed again and thrown into the washing machine. Cotton cloths are easy enough to buy or make and are softer on babies than wipes or paper towels.

To make your own baby wipes, follow the instructions below. I would suggest using cotton flannel material, but bamboo fabric is good too.

### How to make

- Line up two pieces of fabric and pin together.
- Double check that the fabrics are smooth and aligned properly. Adjust as needed before sewing.
- Sew together by hand or by machine.
- Trim the excess threads.
- Iron the seams open or to one side (depending on the thickness of the fabric) to flatten.

## Baby clothes and toys

Clothing waste is a huge societal problem. Babies grow so quickly that half the clothes you get for them never even get used, so charity shops are often full of brand-new baby clothes. Combining charity-shop finds with hand-me-downs from friends and family, means that you hardly ever have to buy new clothes for your baby.

There are also some really great new initiatives for baby clothes swaps, so we don't have to buy any new clothes. The way it works is you sign up and get a delivery of your first set of clothes, 0 to 3 months. Once the baby reaches the next growth level you send back all the 0 to 3 months' clothes and get the next stage, 3 to 6 months and so on.

Babies get tired of toys quickly, so see if friends have toys you can use or do a toy swap with your baby group. Once again, the charity shops will have some great pre-loved items. Check to see if you have a local toy library where you can go and borrow toys for a few weeks at a time. There are many 'freecycles' online where you can find pre-loved toys, clothes and everything in between for your baby. It is also fun to have a toy swap with other parents.

## Baby food

Now for baby food! This can be one of those swaps that is easier than you may think. As a business owner I don't have a lot of spare time, but if I do just a little bit at the weekend I can be organised for the week ahead. I buy most of my fruit and veg at the local market. Items that I can't get from there I will go to my local 'loose' shop. There are many simple recipes that you can make and freeze at the weekend that don't have long prep times. Even just steaming a variety of loose veg, mashing it and freezing it can work.

### Banana Oatmeal Cookies

This is one of the easiest foods that I have put together for Flo. Banana cookies can be made with anything you have to hand, they can be frozen and are very nutritious for your little one.

### How to make

- Mash two bananas (the riper they are, the sweeter and easier they are to mash).
- Add about 1 cup of oats and mix.
- Add in anything else you like (raisins, chopped nuts, coconut, spices, grated courgette or carrot, etc.).
- Form into cookies (these will not flatten when you bake them, so flatten and shape them before they go into the oven).
- Bake at 180 °C/350 °F for approximately 15 minutes.
- Let them cool, then store them in an airtight container for one to two days or freeze them for up to three months.

These days you can find loads of easy recipes online. I suggest having a look at all the ingredients to see what can be bought without any packaging.

I feel we all need to work together to educate people about single-use plastic and the harm it causes our planet. It is up to every one of us to spread the message, start conversations and talk to our youngsters, because they are the generation that will help us make those small swaps. Nothing is more convincing than seeing the difference you can make.

*Carly Catalano*

Sources
- www.gloucestershirerecycles.com/reduce-your-waste/real-reusable-nappies/
- Baby clothes swap: bundlee.co.uk/pages/how-it-works

# Community Action

# Katharina's story: Atelier

## The Atelier project – a community space and a makers' space

telier Stroud was set up to support textile practice for amateurs and professionals alike. It encourages amateurs and professional makers and crafters to work alongside each other and to share ideas and skills. We have drop-in sessions that invite anyone to come in and use the space. Atelier also provides a platform for a variety of creative work, hosting performance, films, exhibitions, workshops and a variety of community events, such as the Stroud Repair Café. It has become a hub for community activism, with a core of creativity and sustainability. Atelier was set up to provide a convivial environment in which everyday social interaction and more formal modes of discourse and exchange could be nurtured. We recognise that creativity is often the product of social encounter, rather than a special quality of a particular individual.

The 'slow fashion' movement is important to us at Atelier. Carl Honoré, author of *In Praise of Slowness*, explains it well: 'The "slow approach" intervenes as a revolutionary process in the contemporary world because it encourages taking time to ensure quality production, to give value to the product, and contemplate the connection with the environment.'

In a similar way, although Atelier has evolved from the interests and singular vision of an individual (myself), I have discovered that we have moved towards a form of 'distributed' leadership, in which it is not regarded as a skill set or attribute possessed by an individual, but rather as something that arises within the relationships and interactions of many people and the context in which they operate. We try with all our different events to ask makers to share tools and knowledge and develop local access to these resources.

### Atelier

Atelier is something that grew out of a love of making, understanding quality and being part of the local community. For us, living sustainably is rooted in these interests. We found that by showing how this can be done, through teaching and sharing, we are able to communicate ideas of how we as a community can find a more sustainable way of living.

- How things are done (the integrity of a skill)
- Where things come from (the importance of provenance)
- Which and how many resources are used (financial and ecological sustainability)

'We recognise that
creativity is often the
product of social
encounter, rather than
a special quality of a
particular individual.'

# atelier events

## Atelier Club

**Frequency**

Open for everyone six sessions a week. Everyone can turn up and use the space and tools. Attendees pay per session or a monthly membership. We encourage people to turn up with their own projects and share ideas and skills.

## Stroud Repair Café

**Collaborators**

Transition Stroud

**Frequency**

Monthly (Last Saturday every month)

Every last Saturday in the month Atelier opens its door to everyone who wants help with repairs to everyday things. Transition Stroud has a database of repairers that can be called upon for support with skills and tools.

## Stroud District Action on Plastic

**Collaborators**

Transition Stroud, Stroud Action on Plastic, Claudi Williams

**Frequency**

Monthly (Last Saturday every month)

The SDAP meet-up gives people an opportunity to talk about the ongoing initiatives in the district. Ideas are shared and small workshops/demonstrations are run on how to minimise plastic in our daily lives.

## Meet Make Mend

**Stroud darning and mending circle**

**Collaborators**

Katy Bevan, Hawthorn Press, Bristol Textile Quarter, South West England Fibreshed project

**Frequency**

Monthly

- Meet other members of Stroud textile community
- Make new contacts, share skills and start new projects
- Mend a beloved piece of clothing

Bring clothes to mend with your sewing bits and bobs if you have them. There will be people on hand to offer guidance and advice and we will provide extra resources, needles, yarn, thread and fabric to help you mend your beloved old clothes.

## #CultureReset

**Events during a pandemic**

**Collaborators**

Stroud Valley Artspace (SVA), Creative Sustainability

**Frequency**

Monthly

During the early summer of 2020 we (Atelier + SVA) created conversation sessions as part of the Culture Reset project – a UK-wide programme to inspire more relevant and impactful cultural community practices, inspired by the urgent need to accelerate change and respond to the experiences of a broader diversity of people and an ecological collapse. Since September 2020 we have invited the Stroud (and wider) community to join us in discussions with a local focus.

# make a space

## Cosmopolitan localism

Stroud is an active community when it comes to concern about environmental and social issues. That spirit was one of the main inspirations for creating Atelier and has steered our development. Various community projects have made Atelier their home, such as the monthly Repair Café, Stroud's Wikithon, Action on Plastic meet-ups and our Meet, Make and Mend darning circle.

## A network of spaces and skill sharing with other community projects

In spring 2019 Atelier initiated a collaborative events programme, 'Creative Spaces Making Communities'. This project highlighted how spaces and projects interact with their communities. Atelier is interested in exploring the various roles played by creative spaces – in providing workspace, support and shared resources for artists and craftspeople, but also in community building, place-making and as hubs for the exchange of knowledge and experience. As part of this project we (Stroud Valley Arts and Atelier) were lucky enough to be able to work together with projects from Berlin that came to Stroud to explain their setup, what made them successful and what kind of challenges they are facing. We found that 'cosmopolitan localism' doesn't only belong in academic papers. We saw that matching the local with the global is good for all of us, helping us to be more aware of the consequences of our actions.

*Katharina Child*
www.atelierstroud.co.uk

### A recipe for space making: creative spaces, creating communities

- Create a regular meeting place
  Make it available online live or recorded
- Create collaborations with like-minded initiatives locally and on a national (and maybe even international) level
- Map the initiatives
- Create events and workshops that exemplify the ethos for the initiatives

# knitted dishcloth patterns

Knitted in washable cotton, these flannels or dishcloths provide a sustainable alternative to disposable wet wipes or kitchen cloths. Use double knit cotton, or two finer 4ply strands, and 4.5–5mm (US size 6/7) needles. Tension isn't important – it's just a cloth after all, so a great project to learn and experiment with. These patterns are just combinations of knit and purl, you can make up your own. Ours came out at about 22 x 24cm (8½ x 9½in) square. Wash them regulary with the rest of your load, they get more absorbent the more they are washed.

### Cloth 1 – Garter stitch

Suitable for beginners.

Cast on about 40–50 stitches. Knit until you have a square, then cast off and sew in ends. Enjoy!

### Cloth 2 – Moss stitch

Cast on 46 stitches.

Row 1: *k1, p1, rep from * to end.

Row 2: *p1, k1, rep from * to end.

Repeat these 2 rows approx 36 times [76 rows] or until your washcloth is square.

Cast off and sew in ends.

### Cloth 3 – Double moss stitch

If you've knitted before.

Cast on 46 sts.

Row 1: *k2, p2* rep to end.

Row 2: rep row 1.

Row 3: *p2, k2*, rep to end.

Row 4: rep row 2.

These 4 rows form the pattern. Rep a further 16 times or until your washcloth is square.

Cast off and sew in ends.

### Cloth 4 – Waffle stitch

Cast on 47 stitches.

Row 1: *k2, p1*, rep to last 2 sts, k2.

Row 2: *p2, k1*, rep to last 2 sts, p2.

Rows 3 and 4: Knit.

These 4 rows form the pattern, rep a further 16 times or until your washcloth is square.

Cast off and sew in ends.

## Cloth 5 – Cable stitch

May require concentration.

You will need a cable needle or a cocktail stick for this pattern

Cast on 56 sts.

Row 1: p4, *k4, p2, rep from * to last 4 sts, p4 [right side].

Row 2: k4, *p4, k2, rep from * to last 4 sts, k4.

Row 3: p4, *k4, p2, rep from * to last 4 sts, p4.

Row 4: k4, *p4, k2, rep from * to last 4 sts, k4.

Row 5: p4,* drop the next 2 sts or place on a cable needle or cocktail stick, hold at front of work, k2, pick up and k2 at front, p2*, rep to last 4 sts, p4.

Rep rows 1–4, then rows 1–2 again (6 rows) then rep the cabling (row 5). This row is repeated every 7th row. If you don't have a cable needle, you can improvise or just drop the stitches and pick them up again.

## Cloth 6 – Garter stitch diagonal

Easy when you know how.

Increase 1 stitch at the beginning of each row by knitting into the front and back of the same stitch (kfb).

Cast on 3 sts.

Row 1: k1, kfb, k1 [4sts].

Row 2: k1, kfb, knit to end.

Repeat last row until one side measures approx 20cm (8in), or the size you want, then begin decreases.

K1, SSK (that is, slip 1 st as if to knit, slip next in the same way, insert needle into the back and knit them together, or you can just k2 tog if you prefer). Repeat the last row until you have 3 sts, then cast off.

### Make a loop

Using the end of the yarn and a crochet hook, make a chain of 12 and work the last st back into the cloth. Turn and work dc into the ring until full, then sew the ends into the cloth to secure.

# Paul's story: Repair Café

**Paul Hofman, a director at Transition Stroud, helps run the Nailsworth Repair Café**

rowing up in the 1950s and 1960s, I remember having few toys, yet spending a lot of time playing and having no shortage of things to play with. One early memory from about four years old is of my parents taking me along for Sunday tea to a friend who was a clockmaker and repairer. I must have shown some fascination for what he did, as each time we visited, I would leave with a clock or something mechanical.

I was intrigued by the mechanics and soon learned that the best way to understand how things work was to take them apart. Putting things back together wasn't really an option, but the bits I collected were my playthings. I recombined them into strange mechanical hybrids like the ones in *Toy Story* – it's called repurposing now, then I was making my own toys.

I moved onto radios, typewriters, motors and anything else that was broken, not realising that I was learning a lot about engineering and how things worked. It wasn't unusual for me to have a Christmas or birthday present and a few months later for it to be taken apart or adapted. I had to discover what was going on inside.

My mum, dad and extended family were always making or fixing things and working with primary materials – cloth, wool, timber, metal, concrete. The messages living in this family were simple: if you wanted something enough, then you could make it; if something broke, you could fix it. Like most kids, I grew up thinking that what my parents did was what everyone's parents did.

I wrote to my dad shortly before he died in 1993 thanking him for some of the things he had done for me – making sure I mentioned all the junk that he'd brought home for me to play with.

As a family, it's still what we do. One cold and rainy Easter Monday, three generations gathered around the table. My 92-year-old mum was looking at a YouTube video on how to replace the screen for a smartphone. My daughter was labelling the parts as we took the phone apart. Six of us were engaged and contributing to a successful repair, all of us feeling good when the phone recovered, and its screen glowed back into life.

‘The messages living in this family were simple: if you wanted something enough, then you could make it; if something broke, you could fix it.’

'We know that once you've mended one thing, you're likely to change the way you see the things that are broken.'

## Repair Cafés

The Repair movement was the brainchild of Martine Postma in 2009. At the time of writing, according to the Repair Café International Foundation she founded in Amsterdam, there are over 2,090 Repair Cafés worldwide, and that's just the ones registered with them. The Foundation offers a manual containing all the information you need to start your own local Repair Café, though many people are just doing it for themselves. The cafes become a local hub for sharing skills and advice, keeping things out of landfill as well as getting people to mix and socialise within their communities. Find your local one and take along that old toaster to get fixed, or volunteer your own skills to help others.

Taking real things apart exposes you to the complexity of engineering – often many simple, understandable parts linked together by gears, belts, wires and chains to achieve something very complicated. A lot of what I came into contact with then was electromechanical, rather than electronic. It was more obvious which bits did what – less so with the sealed black boxes of today. Trying to understand how things work gives you an insight into the intelligent (or otherwise) solutions designers and engineers have come up with. Of course, all this is hidden away unless you take the lid off. This early hands-on engagement with things showed itself later as I took up physics, chemistry and maths at school – living subjects to me, as I could see their relevance and application in the real world.

Repair Cafés started in the Netherlands in 2010. In conjunction with Transition Stroud, I set up the Nailsworth Repair Café at the Sub Rooms in Nailsworth near Stroud, because I enjoyed (and thought I was good at) fixing things. I also wanted to share an enthusiasm for how things worked.

The Repair Café runs on a simple model that does what it says on the tin. The repair part – people

bring in anything that's broken (yes anything – an Italian wall clock, a coffee grinder, the inevitable toasters and kettles). There, you'll usually find enthusiastic volunteers who are only too happy to help you fix what's broken. The café part is tea, coffee and biscuits.

For some people, it's the first time they've ever removed a few screws and looked inside anything. Often we assume that if we break something, we have to find an expert to fix it. Finding those experts can be tough, prohibitively expensive and they may recommend that you just buy a new one. That's the narrative, true or not. We delegate tasks that seem complicated, but in the Repair Café, we can work together, pooling skills and ideas, tools and materials.

A Repair Café can sometimes seem like an A&E department. People are very attached to the things that no longer work. We use a triage process, some

people don't want to be present at the operation but need reassurance that everything will be okay in the end, though sometimes it's not. The good news is that about three-quarters of what comes in gets mended.

At a Repair Café, 'fixers' will take you on a journey to appreciate how the thing you want to fix works and maybe suggest why it's not working. Sometimes it's obvious what's wrong, and you might need some advice on what sort of glue to use. Fixing it is the creative part – you're not always going to have the exact part to replace, and you might have to improvise or repurpose something else.

Fixing something you thought you couldn't fix is usually a very satisfying experience. We know that once you've mended one thing, you're likely to change the way you see items that are broken. It gets us to question the habit of dumping anything that's broken.

We all waste resources, and we do so through well-trodden paths of habit – remember the free plastic bags at the supermarket checkout? We habitually buy, consume and throw away, believing that if it's broken, it can't be fixed and must be binned and replaced. Repair Cafés alone won't make much difference to what we throw away, however they can help us question and break the habits of a lifetime.

To reduce the amount of waste we make, we need to understand more the things we own, and how to maintain and repair them. We need to be less concerned with the surface appearance of things, and be happy if they show signs of wear, tear and repair.

*Paul Hofman*
transitionstroud.org

## Fix the planet

Electronic waste is the toxic legacy of our digital age says iFixit the online directory for the fixing community. The chemicals used in electronic devices, such as computers and mobile phones, are some of the most toxic and hard to recycle. The answer: use your kit for as long as you can and fix it. iFixit's Repair Manifesto is a call to arms to promote the right to mend and prevent the built-in obsolescence that is so prevalent.

# Shalize's story: Madia & Matilda

I started Madia & Matilda in 2013 after studying fashion: the brain child of my university degree. I hated the waste created by pattern cutting and couldn't understand why so much material would be discarded. My design projects were all concerned with sustainability. I remember thinking, 'why is this the norm, why can't I save this material for something else?' Or 'If I cut in the opposite direction would I not save more material?' And, 'What else could it be used for?'

Having witnessed at firsthand how the fashion industry works, I decided to make small steps to change the way we shop. In this way, sustainability has become the founding ethos of my new business.

The brand is now known for its pop-ups and commitment to the environment. Based in the Stroud area, Madia & Matilda features on online retailer sites such as SilkFred and ASOS. We have recently joined Vegan Threads, an online marketplace dedicated to vegan fashion, and

Clearpay, a layaway payment provider – a sort of deposit scheme with fee, when you pay a deposit and pay off the item over time – making the cost of sustainable fashion affordable for those who may not otherwise be able to afford it. In the future we are looking at ways to partner with companies that can calculate the cost of carbon consumption per garment, making the impact of their purchases more transparent to the consumer.

My approach to running a small independent business is to combine my passion for sustainability and the environment with our office practices; craftsmanship with the minimalism and functionality of modern design. We are dedicated to crafting pieces from upcycled and sustainable materials into luxury garments that outlast trends and seasons while making a positive impact on the planet at every stage in the process. All our materials are end of line, vintage or offcuts, so we are stopping materials from going to landfill. We use end-of-line materials or materials that have tiny defects – otherwise they would be thrown away. With a strong belief in conscious

'WRAP's consumer research has found that on average, clothing lasts for 3.3 years before it is discarded or passed on and worldwide, clothing utilisation – the average number of times a garment is worn before it ceases to be used – has decreased by 36% compared to 15 years ago.'
Source: WRAP, Valuing Our Clothes – The Cost of UK Fashion, 2017, www.wrap.org.uk/sites/files/wrap/valuing-our-clothes-the-cost-of-uk-fashion_WRAP.pdf

'Despite improvements in the carbon footprint per tonne, the total footprint of clothing in use in the UK, including global and territorial emissions, was 26.2 million tonnes of $CO_2e$ in 2016, up from 24 million tonnes in 2012.'
Source: WRAP, Valuing Our Clothes – The Cost of UK Fashion, 2017, www.wrap.org.uk/sites/files/wrap/valuing-our-clothes-the-cost-of-uk-fashion_WRAP.pdf

## Fast Fashion

Creating fashion with a positive impact and early establishment of eco-friendly practices resonates with younger generations of shoppers. Sustainability is increasingly becoming a selling point. Eco-related keywords in product descriptions are being increasingly used, according to *The Edited*. Mentions of 'sustainable' rose 16% from 2017 to 2018, with 'eco' up 24%, 'vegan' up 25% and 'recycled' up 35% year on year.

'The highest contributor to the carbon footprint of clothing is the production of fibre through polymer extrusion or agriculture.'

Source: WRAP, Valuing Our Clothes – The Cost of UK Fashion, 2017, www.wrap.org.uk/sites/files/wrap/valuing-our-clothes-the-cost-of-uk-fashion_WRAP.pdf

consumption, sustainability is deeply ingrained in our business practice, from the way we cut our fabrics to the materials we source, vintage, secondhand or dead stock, and all our processes show our commitment to sustainable fashion. We also create garments in smaller batches to avoid the waste of unsold items.

Our designs are timeless, combined with reworking, and we have created a special style that goes hand in hand with sustainability. All our ranges are produced biannually. These are the first steps towards a list of very ambitious, long-term goals. With each item, we carefully consider our design, material and production process for a greater impact on your wardrobe and a smaller impact on the environment, with better-quality pieces that our customers will love and treasure for years to come.

Our ethos is to keep resources in use for as long as possible and we are constantly striving to be better by improving our processes, working with recycling centres and providing alterations in-store, which also helps to lower consumer impact. With people becoming more aware of their consumer power, there is a growing movement of change, dedicated to combating waste and the throwaway culture.

This year, we're celebrating seven years of Madia & Matilda. We are growing and our designs are now sold all over the world, and it's great to see the reach. We are committed to circular design principles and creating apparel using easy to care for, non-toxic fabrications from renewable resources that are recyclable. With a zero waste commitment at heart, we've created a business model that is sustainable and ready for whatever the future brings.

*Shalize Nicholas*
www.madiamatilda.co.uk

‘Less than 1% of material used to produce clothing is recycled into new clothing, representing a loss of more than USD 100 billion worth of materials each year, and only 13% of the total material input is in some way recycled after clothing use.’

Source: Ellen MacArthur Foundation, A new textiles economy: Redesigning fashion's future, 2017, www.ellenmacarthurfoundation.org/publications.

# Managing domestic waste

umans, like many mammals, have always produced waste. Dumps of human feeding remains or middens, as archaeologists call them, date back to the Stone Age when our hunter gatherer ancestors began to live in more settled communities, exploiting freshwater mussels, oysters, clams and whelks.

The process of repurposing waste has been common practice throughout history in order to conserve materials and maximise output. Since 1971 when Friends of the Earth returned thousands of empties to the London HQ of Cadbury Schweppes calling for bottle recycling, the act of putting out your weekly recycling has been synonymous with being 'green' and 'doing your bit for the environment'. Indeed, there are carbon emission savings to be made by recycling nearly all materials (see chart on page 77). Aluminium drinks cans made of recycled aluminium can save over 8,000kg $CO_2e$ ($CO_2e$ = carbon dioxide equivalent) per tonne of aluminium compared to using bauxite ore. While recycling is definitely a very good thing, it is not the whole answer, so this doesn't mean we can then be profligate with our limited resources. In order to offset the carbon emissions of just one return flight to New York, 8,500 aluminium drinks cans would need to be recycled and that's a lot of canned drinks.

Waste collection and recycling are one of the services provided by local authorities that are used by just about every citizen; so getting it right is essential for local politicians who want to get reelected. The ugly side of recycling is the big noisy lorries and recycling crews working their socks off in all weathers. No matter how many people wash out their yogurt pots beforehand, it is a dirty, smelly business and those operatives taking away our leftovers, whatever the weather or national crisis, should have our respect.

There wasn't much plastic before the 1950s and now it is everywhere. Plastic is often seen as an environmental villain and, having worked in the Antarctic I have seen firsthand the devastating

## Recycling success

Stroud District Council received an accolade for Cutting Waste to Landfill in 2019 when the council was identified by the Department for Environment, Food and Rural Affairs (Defra) as the highest performing council for recycling in the south west, with residents throwing away the least amount of residual waste in England. Defra figures show that Stroud district residents lead the way in England, putting out an average of just 258.6kg of residual waste per household in 2017/18 and achieved a 61.2% household recycling rate – up a massive 15.7% on the previous year.

> 'Crisp packets have three to four layers of plastic and foil, including the print and lacquering. A springy type of toothpaste tube can have up to 14 layers of different plastic, including the print and lacquering. Many items such as cleaning spray bottles are made up of multiple types of plastic and it is usual that only one component can be recovered for recycling.'

Source: Tricia Watson, Resource Management Analyst, Director Community R4C

impact of discarded plastic on fur seals, penguins and albatrosses. However, plastic, if used correctly, is an amazing material, responsible for saving millions from food poisoning. It is strong, light, long lasting, and, given the right incentives and facilities, can be recycled. However, carrying a large amount of air-filled plastic to the nearest recycling plant is perhaps not always the best use of fuel and much of it never gets that far.

Most plastic can only be recycled once sorted into the different polymers, and then only once or twice before the material degrades. Sorting is mainly done mechanically, with the addition of a manual sort to ensure all contaminants and those tricky black plastic trays have been removed. Once sorted and cleaned, plastic can either be shredded into flakes or melt processed to form pellets before finally being moulded into new products. The final use, be it another milk bottle, fence post or piece of clothing, is dependent on global markets and particularly on the price of oil; as the price of oil goes up it is cheaper to recycle plastic. It is still far better to put plastic out for recycling than for incineration or to throw it away.

Most of the plastic collected by Stroud District Council is recycled in the UK, mainly because the residents of the district are so diligent in their recycling habits, washing and sorting, resulting in a very low contamination rate. Glass can, in theory, be recycled almost indefinitely, but how

## Plastic facts

'We estimate that 8300 million metric tons (Mt) of virgin plastics have been produced to date. As of 2015, approximately 6300 Mt of plastic waste had been generated, around 9% of which had been recycled, 12% was incinerated, and 79% was accumulated in landfills or the natural environment. If current production and waste management trends continue, roughly 12,000 Mt of plastic waste will be in landfills or in the natural environment by 2050.'

### Reference

Production, use and fate of all plastics ever made, Roland Geyer, Jenna R. Jambeck and Kara Lavender Law. July 2017, University of Santa Barbara and Oxford University, https://advances.sciencemag.org/content/3/7/e1700782

many bottles containing your favourite wine that you bought recently were made from recycled glass? While a proportion of glass is turned back into bottles, most glass sent for recycling is crushed and reused for a variety of purposes from the sparkle in kitchen worktops to aggregates for roads. Even for the latter there are carbon emissions savings over quarried rock.

Pouring wine from a glass bottle, always somehow feels better than from a box or a Tetra Pak, but here the environmental impacts of the container get murky and are not quite as straightforward as glass recycling. Tetra Paks can be recycled, the card being very valuable, although the plastic and metal linings are more difficult to deal with. Then there is the added issue of the weight of the bottles for transporting your favourite Chardonnay or Rioja compared to the minimal weight of a box or Tetra Pak and the fact that one can stack many more litre boxes of wine into a shipping container than glass bottles. Overall, the carbon footprint of wine in bottles is five times greater than that in boxes or Tetra Paks.

Other than using oak casks, probably the most environmentally friendly way to transport wine long distances is in large reuseable plastic containers to be decanted in the supermarket or bar into your own favourite reusable container. I still have a sports drink bottle, which I bought for a cycle touring trip to Spain in 1990, that has been used for water, fruit juice, Gloucestershire cider and even red wine from plastic barrels in Andalucían bars. While recycling is far better than incineration, reuse is, in the long term, even better.

*Simon Pickering is a Stroud District Councillor and Chair of the Environment Committee*

## Polymers and what can't be recycled

'Most plastics can only be recycled once, at which point they are normally converted into clothing or some other commodity which can't be recycled again.'
Source:
Envirotech-Online www.envirotech-online.com/news/environmental-laboratory/7/breaking-news/how-many-times-can-plastic-be-recycled/46064

190 billion Tetra Pak boxes were made in 2019, the majority for milks and juices. The ubiquitous cardboard carton is actually made from several layers of virgin paper, aluminium and plastic, or polyal, requiring specialist equipment to recycle, hence 60–70% of Tetra Pak cartons end up in landfill. Until the production chain is more sustainable, they are still not an ideal solution.

### References

• Turner, D.A., Williams, I.D, and Kemp, S. 'Greenhouse gas emission factors for recycling of source-segregated waste materials' in Resources, Conservation and Recycling Vol. 105, Part A, December 2015, 186–97

• Mike Berners-Lee, *How bad are Bananas? The Carbon footprint of everything*, Profile Books, 2010

• Schmidt, C. Krauth, O.T. Wagner, S. 2017 'Export of Plastic Debris by Rivers into the Sea' Environmental Science and Technology 2017, 51, 21, 12,246–12,253

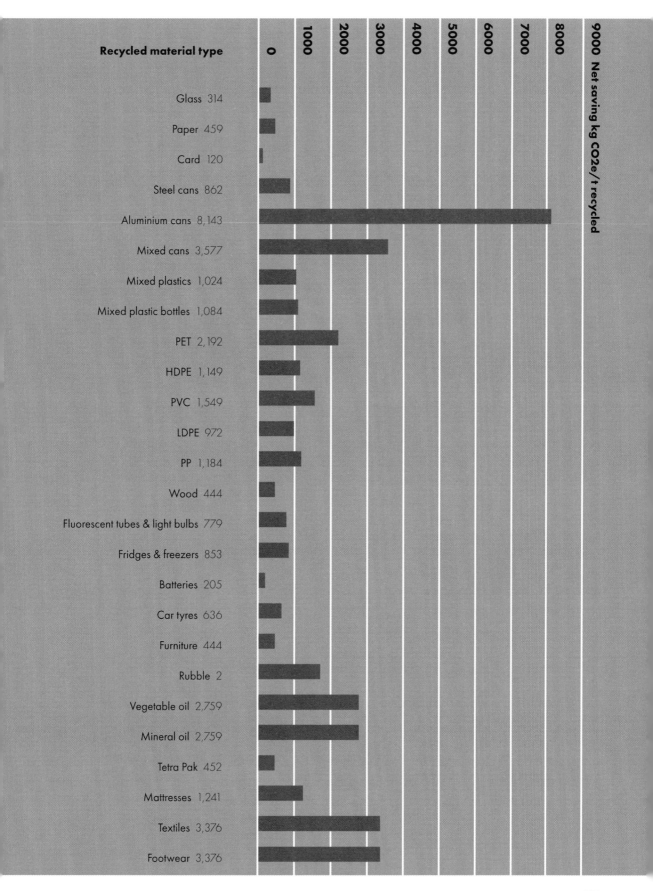

**Recycled material type**

**Net saving kg CO2e/t recycled**

|  |  |
|---|---|
| Glass | 314 |
| Paper | 459 |
| Card | 120 |
| Steel cans | 862 |
| Aluminium cans | 8,143 |
| Mixed cans | 3,577 |
| Mixed plastics | 1,024 |
| Mixed plastic bottles | 1,084 |
| PET | 2,192 |
| HDPE | 1,149 |
| PVC | 1,549 |
| LDPE | 972 |
| PP | 1,184 |
| Wood | 444 |
| Fluorescent tubes & light bulbs | 779 |
| Fridges & freezers | 853 |
| Batteries | 205 |
| Car tyres | 636 |
| Furniture | 444 |
| Rubble | 2 |
| Vegetable oil | 2,759 |
| Mineral oil | 2,759 |
| Tetra Pak | 452 |
| Mattresses | 1,241 |
| Textiles | 3,376 |
| Footwear | 3,376 |

# Protect the Earth

## The Earth Protector movement

aybe it was my father, who got me out of bed on a summer's eve to go and look for wild flowers; or maybe it was picnicking in the beech woods, when he cooked tinned spaghetti in a camping kettle and poured it out of the spout. What is it in us that nurtures a love of nature?

I recall once asking that question round a table of community gardener friends. Each one responded with a childhood memory of magical moments in nature with a family member: influences that have stayed with us. For PLUs, or people like us, therefore, the current unravelling state of our Earth and the threat of collapse to our ecosystems, is inadmissible and unbearable. I spent many years feeling powerless, until I met someone who taught me by her own example that if you believe

you can make a difference you will. And that changed my attitude and my life.

That someone was Polly Higgins, widely known as the Earth lawyer, who dedicated her life to finding a legally binding way to protect the Earth. Polly often spoke of a critical choice point that arrives in our lives. We can choose to remain safe with what we know or step out into the unknown. For Polly this was daring to be great, which she later wrote a book about, *Dare to be Great*.

One day when she was defending a client who had suffered deep harm, Polly reflected that the Earth similarly suffers grave injury but has no one to defend her: 'The Earth needs a good lawyer,' she thought and with that, her critical choice was set: to give up a successful career to defend one client only, the Earth.

*The current unravelling state of our Earth and the threat of collapse to ecosystems, is inadmissible and unbearable.*

I had given much time and effort over the years to the Transition Town movement, inspired by Rob Hopkins. Anita Roddick had influenced me with her ethical, fair trade model for social justice in business. My next heroine was American activist Joanna Macy with her *Active Hope* book, co-authored with Chris Johnstone, which connects us all with our pain and our power to act at this planetary moment.

But when it came to Polly, my critical choice point arrived and I did not need to think twice. I wrote to ask her if I could help. I am not a lawyer. I had no idea what I could offer. I did not expect a reply from one so globally involved with just about the most important job I could imagine: to find a way to protect the Earth. She did reply. So after 20 years of living in Sussex, when most retired people (like me) of a respectable age would be well settled, I rented out my house (cat included), and explained to all my Transition friends of many years that I was leaving to help Polly Higgins. Three months later I moved to Stroud. Like many others, for years I had arduously

recycled, taught my kids to be eco-aware, campaigned for this and protested about that, organised workshops in schools to save the whale, cleaned beaches, made our own cardboard Christmas tree, bicycled into town despite the rain, as well as investing ethically.

Immediately, I was plunged into the deep waters of ecocide, the serious loss or mass destruction of Earth's ecosystems. The enormous, courageous undertaking of Polly's vision to address this devastation overwhelmed me with the sheer enormity of the task. Polly had rigorously developed a law which would declare ecocide a crime and hold the perpetrators accountable.

Once I understood the potential of this to stop the harm and realistically bring in the changes needed, I became inspired and powerful. I spoke to everyone at every possible opportunity. Polly called it 'seeding': spreading the word, raising awareness. At first I was greeted with disbelief: 'that'll never happen,' 'no one can get a law like that past all the powerful interests,' and so on. I

Polly Higgins: photo Ruth Davey www.look-again.org

kept talking. The more I believed I could get over the message I so deeply cared about, the more I succeeded. The arguments and the stares of disbelief lessened.

Meanwhile, the planetary crisis deepened until the shock reality hit the headlines, first with the Intergovernmental Panel on Climate Change (IPCC) report and over the last year with ever more apocalyptic events, from fires to floods to links between habitat destruction and the origins of the COVID pandemic. Official interest in a law of ecocide is emerging from Vanuatu to the Vatican and from France to Finland. This development is supported by a growing number of individual Earth Protectors who have signed up to fund its progress.

This has generated a more local small-scale response, the Earth Protector Communities, aiming to contribute to protecting the Earth by seeking to minimise small, daily harmful impacts. An Earth Protector Town starts with the town council setting the intention to make all policy decisions from the principle of: 'First do no harm,' to protect land, water, air, soil and wildlife. Businesses, schools and community organisations are invited to follow the guidelines in a self-authorising exploration to identify areas in which to improve: to create desired targets and action plans in order to reach a regenerative outcome. There is much to do; the aim is a global network of Earth Protector Towns, businesses, schools, universities and other organisations: in short, global Earth Protector Communities.

Can I believe strongly enough that this CAN and WILL happen? This is a choice.

Yes, I can and yes, I will.

It is daring to be great and stepping into the potential we each uniquely hold to be the hope for the world we know is possible. I thank Polly for her remarkable life and for her legacy work for our Earth.

*Anita van Rossum*

- *Dare to be Great: Unlock Your Power to Create a Better World*, Polly Higgins, was republished by The History Press in April 2020 on the anniversary of her death.
- *Eradicating Ecocide: Laws and governance to Prevent the Destruction of Our Planet*, by Polly Higgins 2nd Edition (2015).

**www.stopecocide.earth**
**www.earthprotectorcommunities.net**

> ❝Greatness is a predilection for life itself plus a willingness to give of the self in service to something greater than all of life itself.❞
>
> Polly Higgins (1968–2019)

# stop ecocide

Ecocide is the mass damage and destruction of ecosystems, widespread or severe or systematic. It is serious harm to nature, committed with knowledge of the risks.

The Earth Protector movement springs from the work of the late Polly Higgins, the Earth Lawyer, who dedicated her life to finding a legally binding way to protect the Earth.

Earth Protectors contribute to a ring-fenced fund. This finances the legal and diplomatic work required to progress the tabling of an amendment to the Rome Statute to include Ecocide as an international crime alongside Genocide and Crimes Against Humanity.

Once in place, the Law of Ecocide will hold a corporate director or government minister accountable and Ecocide will become an international crime. This will totally change the current situation of impunity in which no one is held responsible. The continuous cycle of destruction will be halted, prohibited and prevented. Corporations can continue to profit, but not at the cost of the Earth; nor the safety, health and future of all life. It is our responsibility, each and every one of us, to do what we can to stop ecocide, the overwhelming threat to all life on Earth.

The Earth Protector movement promotes the campaign to STOP ECOCIDE: change the law. Becoming an Earth Protector is the first single most important thing you can do right now. Spread the word, set up Earth Protector Hubs in your area. Bring people together over this vital issue. The Stop Ecocide team will support and resource you. Get in touch. We are all in this together. We must act together. Sign up to become an Earth Protector to fund the one law that can stop the harm and protect our Earth.

Current number of Earth Protectors: 18,271
International Petition to support making ecocide a crime: 24,100 signatures

Earth Protector Communities are another vital way for Earth Protectors to engage on a local level. Earth Protector Towns, with the town council heading up the intention, is currently a pilot project in Stroud. Other towns are registering their interest. Find out and get involved.
(See www.earthprotectorcommunities.net)
It won't just be the law that changes, but the whole course of human history.

www.stopecocide.earth

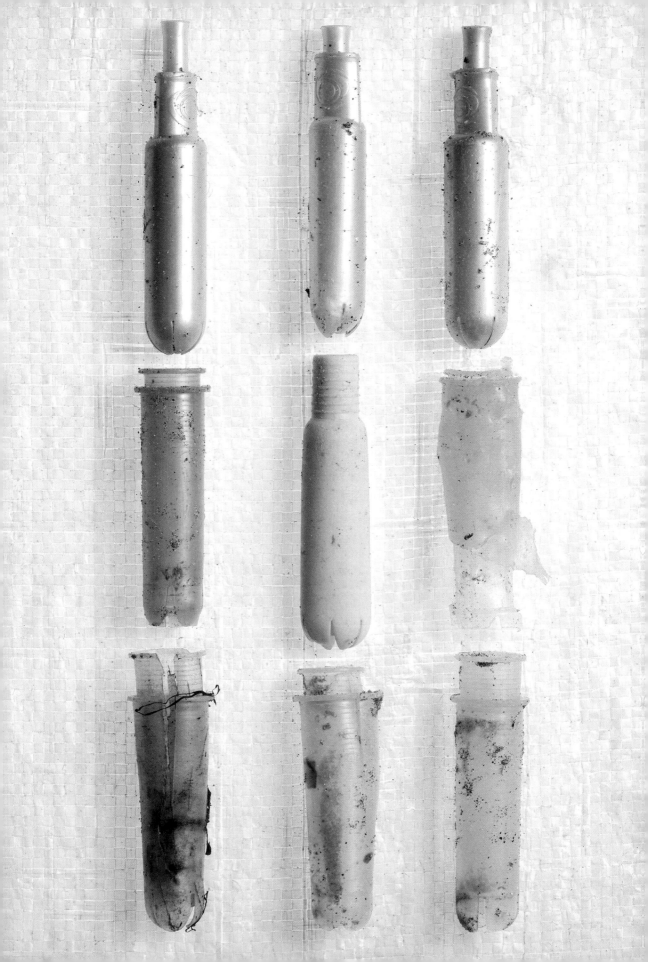

# Individual Action

# Making a plastic audit

If you feel inspired to start your own plastic-free journey, it is helpful to start with a plastic audit of your home to find out where you can make changes with the most impact. Most of us are unaware of how much plastic we have accumulated and so this bit can be a bit overwhelming but at the same time it might help to strengthen your resolve.

## Audit of your kitchen, food buying and cleaning methods

Consider all the items in your kitchen, from the contents of your fridge and freezer, your larder, food storage and preparation area to what is under your sink.

Do you buy plastic bottles and Tetra Paks of milk, water, fizzy drinks etc. and could you switch to refillable alternatives (for example, from Milk & More) or obtained in refillable containers? Could you make your own plant milk? Could you get a soda stream for fizzy drinks?

Do you consider the packaging when you buy in other food supplies – is there anything that could be supplied unpackaged or in reduced/paper packaging, or in glass or in your own containers?

When buying fresh fruit and veg, do you have a good supply of your own fabric bags and containers that you can take shopping so you can avoid prepackaged food and thin plastic produce bags? Have you considered buying at farm shops or markets?

Do you buy sauces and condiments in plastic bottles and could you switch to making your own or in glass bottles, for example tomato sauce and salad dressings?

Could sweets be bought in bulk and then divided into reusable containers (mugs, bowls or jars etc.) rather than individual small packets? Could you buy them unpackaged from a sweet shop perhaps?

Could your tea/coffee be supplied to you plastic free, for example directly from a local supplier, a plastic-free/zero waste shop near you or a plastic free bulk store online?

If you buy frozen and ready meals, have you considered plastic-free alternatives and avoiding items shrink-wrapped in plastic, like pizza. Consider buying loose frozen food like frozen peas at garden centres and farm shops.

Are your sponges and other kitchen cleaning kit made of plastic (microfibre cloths, for example, which shed tiny plastic fibres into the water supply)? Alternatives made from wood, bamboo, loofah or coconut fibre are now widely available in shops and online – could you swap for plastic free?

Are disposable wipes (which are largely composed of plastic) used in cleaning? Can these be eliminated in favour of reusable cloths?

Are your dishwasher tablets wrapped in plastic? Could these be swapped for an alternative supplied in cardboard, such as your supermarket's own brand?

Could washing up liquid bottles be refilled at a refill suppliers near you, rather than bought new each time (look for Ecoleaf, Ecover and Bio-D refill places). Or could you use Ocean Saver/Dropshot/similar soluble cleaning sachets, that are used to top up a spray bottle? If this is not feasible for some reason, could you use products that come in packaging made from recycled materials (e.g. Ecover) and buy in bulk to reduce packaging? Similarly, kitchen cleaning products. Could you cut down on the number of products you use or even make your own?

Are your bin bags biodegradable? If you live in an area where food waste is collected by your council, your landfill bin might not need a liner at all.

If you still use clingfilm for food preservation, could beeswax wraps be used as an alternative?

**Audit of your bathroom**
Consider toiletries in your bathroom and showers as well as the cleaning products.

Could you cut down on the number of cleaning products and could your containers be refilled, or at least supplied in bottles made from recycled materials and bought in bulk to reduce packaging? Could you make some of your own cleaning products? Could you switch to using bi-carb, citric acid and borax substitute in cardboard boxes from the hardware store?

Could bars of soap be used instead of liquid, or could hand soap dispensers be refilled rather than having to be replaced?

Could sanitary products come from a plastic free brand (e.g. Natracare) or could you use washable products?

Could nappies be reusable, washable and made from cloth? There are excellent cloth products and nappy washing services available for babies and toddlers and there are sustainable brands for single-use items, suchs as Premier Nappies and Nu Bamboo and more that are sure to follow.

As above, are disposable wipes (which contain a high percentage of plastic) used in cleaning? Can these be eliminated in favour of reusable cloths?

Could you replace other bathroom products that come packaged in single-use plastic with those that don't? For example, could plastic wrapped toilet roll be replaced with the same in paper packaging or a box of 'naked' rolls from Greencane or Who Gives a Crap?

**Continue the audit in other areas:**
- **Clothing**
- **Baby items**
- **Kids toys/school supplies**
- **Stationary supplies**
- **Garden shed and garage**
- **Packed lunches/food on the go**
- **Going on holiday**

# Make a plastic pledge

**W**hen it comes to making a plastic pledge, make sure to keep it simple and achievable. An easy way to start is to phase out what you no longer want over time and replace it with alternatives as the need arises. Even after I stopped buying new plastic bottles of cleaning liquids, we still used up what we had over a long period of time. Be guided by solutions that don't cost the earth and that enhance the quality of your life rather than make things more difficult. Seek out allies in your family and enrol your kids or friends to make it a project that is enjoyable and rewarding. These are some examples that you can pick from to make your own personal plastic pledge.

An approach that works for many people is to pick one category or room in your house per month to transform into a plastic-free zone. See some examples below to inspire you.

**Bathroom**
I will find out where to buy refillable shampoo and shower gel, switch to soap bars, buy bamboo toothbrushes, try out plastic-free toothpaste, make my own deodorant, give up cosmetic wipes and use washable cloths instead.

**Kitchen**
I will find out where to refill oil and vinegar, shop with cloth bags for unpackaged fresh food, stock up on unpackaged dried food such as pasta and rice, make my own snacks and treats.

**Laundry and Cleaning**
I will use washing powder and try essential oil instead of fabric conditioner. I will find out where to get laundry and cleaning product liquid refills. I will use natural sponges and cloths, scourers and washing up brushes. I will source dishwasher tablets that are not packaged in plastic.

**Baby's room**
I will try reusable nappies or a reusable nappy service in my area. I will swap baby wipes for washable cloths. I will buy (maybe even secondhand) clothing and also toys made from natural materials.

**Study**
I will explore secondhand items and repairing instead of buying new equipment. I will source stationary that is not wrapped in plastic (paper, staples, pencils, paper packing tape, etc.).

# plastic pledge

I will give up buying water in plastic bottles and instead use a refillable water bottle / get a water filter / get a soda stream / use water fountains when out and about / download the national refill app, etc.

·

I will buy only loose fruit and veg in reusable and washable fabric bags / reuse paper bags

·

I will buy fresh produce such as bread, cheese, meat, fish in my own containers and fabric bags

·

I will give up buying milk in plastic bottles/Tetra Pak and instead sign up to a milk delivery service, find a milk refill station locally, make my own plant milks

·

I will seek out where l can buy unpackaged food and other items at health food shops, zero waste shops, farm shops and markets

·

I will join a local repair café / join a plastic-free community scheme / find like-minded people

·

*Signed*

.......................................................................

Other ways of making a plastic pledge include joining
Plastic Free July, Friends of the Earth,
Surfers Against Sewage's Plastic Free Communities,
Plastic Free Schools, National Geographic plastic pledge
and Greenpeace, amongst others.

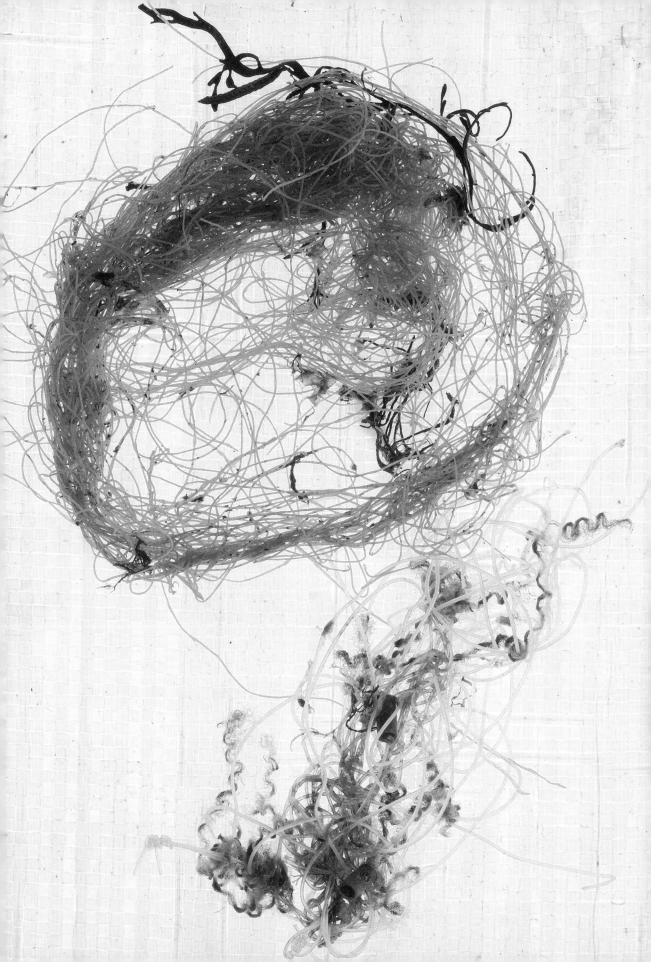

# Good to know

## Collective action

The significant impact of The Everyday Plastic Survey was illustrated after one trial session at which a participant brought in 32 individual pieces of Hello Fresh packaging amongst her week's collection. I tweeted a picture to highlight the stark consequences this could have given their wide customer base.

This simple tweet generated huge traction online and offline, including:

- Hundreds of comments from former and prospective customers
- Press coverage in MailOnline and Daily Mirror
- Hello Fresh statement as a direct response
- Over 7,000 engagements on social media, with the original tweet seen over 650,000 times

**Source:** Daniel Webb of The Everyday Plastic Project, www.everydayplastic.org

A survey found that around half of respondents who know someone who has given up flying because of climate change say they fly less because of this example. Furthermore, around three quarters say it has changed their attitudes towards flying and climate change in some way. The effects are increased if it is a high-profile person that is known to have given up flying, with around two thirds saying they fly less because of this person, and only 7% saying it has not affected their attitudes

**Source:** Westlake, Steve, 'A Counter-Narrative to Carbon Supremacy: Do Leaders Who Give Up Flying Because of Climate Change Influence the Attitudes and Behaviour of Others?' October 2, 2017, ssrn.com/abstract=3283157

Nearly nine in 10 people (88%) who saw the episode of BBC's *Blue Planet II* about the effect of plastics on our oceans have changed their behaviour since. Sixty percent of us now choose a refillable water bottle and coffee cup more than we did, and Waitrose has seen an 800% increase in questions about plastics from customers.

**Source:** Waitrose & Partners Food & Drink Report 2018–19 waitrose.pressarea.com

The UK was surveyed after the 2015 plastic bag charge came into effect. 1 in 4 used shop provided plastic bags one month before the charge, decreasing to 1 in 10 after six months of the charge. Support for the bag and other waste charges increased by 10% six months after it began. The public supports charges or bans, and support typically increases after they are put in place.

**Source:** seas-at-risk.org

## Fast fashion

WRAP's consumer research has found that, on average, clothing lasts for 3.3 years before it is discarded or passed on and worldwide clothing utilisation – the average number of times a garment is worn before it ceases to be used – has decreased by 36% compared to 15 years ago.

Despite improvements in the carbon footprint per tonne, the total footprint of clothing in use in the UK, including global and territorial emissions, was 26.2 million tonnes $CO_2$ in 2016, up from 24 million tonnes in 2012. The highest contributor to the carbon footprint of clothing is the production of fibre through polymer extrusion or agriculture.

**Source:** WRAP, 'Valuing Our Clothes – The Cost of UK Fashion, 2017', www.wrap.org.uk

## Polymers

Most plastics can only be recycled once, at which point they are normally converted into clothing or some other commodity which can't be recycled again.
Source: www.envirotech-online.com

A wide range of items are now made from recycled plastics, including:

- refuse sacks and carrier bags
- underground drainage systems for homes and national infrastructure
- flower pots, seed trays, watering cans and water butts
- wheel arch liners and bumpers on cars
- damp-proof membranes, guttering and window profiles used in construction
- reusable crates and pallets
- wheel bins and food caddies
- composters and wormeries
- drinks bottles and food trays
- polyester fabric for clothing

Source: www.recyclenow.com

Plastic can be made from fossil-based or bio-based materials. Both can be used to make highly durable, non-biodegradable plastics, or plastics which either biodegrade or compost.

**Fact:** Just because a plastic is made from bio-based sources does not automatically mean it will biodegrade! Only non-biodegradable plastic can be recycled, regardless of whether it is fossil-based or bio-based. Compostable plastics can be composted at industrial scale composting facilities. Some compostable plastics can also be home composted and should be clearly labelled if this is the case. Compostable plastics should not go in with your dry recycling as they cannot be recycled in the same way as non-biodegradable plastic.
Source: www.recyclenow.com

Less than 1% of material used to produce clothing is recycled into new clothing, representing a loss of more than USD 100 billion worth of materials each year, and only 13% of the total material input is in some way recycled after clothing use.
Source: Ellen MacArthur Foundation, 'A new textiles economy'

## What really happens to your recycling
(and why you should wash things first)
Plastics are:

- Sorted by polymer type
- Shredded
- Washed
- Melted
- Pelletised
- Made into new products.

It is a two-stage process:

- Sorting is mainly done automatically with a manual sort to ensure all contaminants have been removed.
- Once sorted and cleaned, plastic can either be shredded into flakes or melt processed to form pellets before finally being moulded into new products.

Putting the right stuff in the right bin is important. The wrong stuff is called contamination and when contaminated loads of recycling are found, it can potentially result in the whole lorry full being sent to landfill.

Top tips to help reduce contamination in your bin:

1 Look out for recycling labels on packaging to help identify whether it is recyclable or not.
2 Leave metal caps and lids on glass jars and bottles

## The circular economy

The EU could benefit by 1.8 trillion if it developed a circular economy that reuses and recycles resources – as opposed to the traditional linear economy of make, use and dispose.
Source: Friends of the Earth, policy.friendsoftheearth.uk

Industry is responsible for around 21% of overall global $CO_2$ emissions. The production of four materials – cement, steel, plastics, and aluminium account for 60% of these emissions.

For plastics, recycling 1 tonne could reduce emissions by 1.1–3.0 tonnes of $CO_2$ compared to producing the same tonne of plastics from virgin fossil feedstock. Recycling therefore cuts not just emissions from energy use, but also those from production processes – which are among the trickiest emissions to address. Furthermore, it is easier to use electricity and other low-carbon energy sources to facilitate recycling, compared to new materials production, and therefore it aligns to the target of a net-zero economy.

When recycling, mixing and downgrading effects are particularly serious problems for plastics, making a large share of used plastics literally worthless. Without fundamental redesign and innovation, about 30% of plastic packaging will never be reused or recycled.

If 'refill' bottle designs and models were to be applied to all bottles in beauty and personal care as well as home cleaning, packaging and transport, savings would represent an 80–85% reduction in greenhouse gas emissions compared to today's traditional single-use bottles.

A good example of a fast-growing renewable material is bamboo. Both living biomass and long-lived bamboo products have the potential to sequester 2.6 tonnes of carbon per acre annually, while offering the compressive strength of concrete and the tensile strength of steel.
Source: Ellen MacArthur Foundation, Completing the Picture: How the Circular Economy Tackles Climate Change (2019) www.ellenmacarthurfoundation.org

3 Empty and rinse all containers.
4 Don't forget to recycle items from all rooms in the house, including shampoo bottles from the bathroom.
5 If in doubt, check before you chuck using the Recycling Locator at recyclenow.com.

Top tips for recycling plastic bottles
- Empty plastic bottles and containers before you recycle
- Give them a quick rinse
- Squash plastic drinks bottles to save space in your recycling container
- Remove pumps from liquid soap and cleaning product bottles as these are not recyclable
Source: Recycle Now, www.recyclenow.com

Do you take the cap off your plastic bottles because you think that it will make it easier for it to be recycled once it reaches the recycling plant? Well, you can start leaving the lids on because it's not true.

The plastic bottles, complete with lids, are ground up and put through a water bath. As the lids are usually made from high-density polyethylene (HDPE) and polypropylene (PP), they tend to float, whereas the plastic bottles, made from PET, are heavier and they will sink. This makes it easy for the different types of material to be separated so they can be recovered and turned into new items.
Source: www.recyclingbins.co.uk

## Food waste

In the decade between 2004 and 2014 food waste per person (in the EU) doubled even as the amount of plastic packaging in food products rose by up to 50%.
Source: www.sustainability-times.com

Growth in the application of plastic packaging has increased alongside the growth in food waste, with Europe's total demand for plastic rising to 49 million tonnes per year, of which 40% is used for packaging.

Preserving food at home without plastic packaging:
- Use reusable bags, mason jars and containers when food shopping and storing food at home.
- Store bread in a cloth bag inside a wooden bread bin, as it

### Sea waste

An estimated 640,000 tonnes of abandoned or lost fishing equipment, or 'ghost gear' enters the ocean every year, equivalent in weight to more than 50,000 double-decker buses. In total, they make up around 10% of the plastic waste in our oceans, entangling and killing marine life.
**Source:** Greenpeace, 'Ghost Gear: The Abandoned Fishing Nets Haunting Our Oceans'

Of the plastic that enters the ocean, 94% ends up on the sea floor. There is now on average an estimated 70kg of plastic in each square kilometre of sea bed.
**Source:** Eunomia, www.eunomia.co.uk

Almost two-thirds of Scottish coastal waters tested by Greenpeace have been found to contain evidence of microplastic pollution.
**Source:** 'Testing the Waters – Microplastics in Scottish Seas', www.greenpeace.org.uk

In a Surfers Against Sewage brand audit of just under 50,000 items found on UK beaches in 2019, 10 parent companies accounted for well over half the total number of items.
**Source:** Surfers Against Sewage, www.sas.org.uk/

absorbs moisture (unlike a plastic bag) and prevents bread from moulding quickly.
- Choose retailers that use minimal packaging and allow food to be bought in bulk.
- Store the stems of leafy vegetables and herbs (e.g., lettuce, celery, parsley, coriander) in water to keep them fresh.
- Understand which fruit and vegetables should be stored at room temperature (e.g., tomatoes and lemons).
- Understand which foods spoil more quickly when wrapped in plastic (e.g., mushrooms, soft cheeses).
- Store apples with potatoes but separate from other fruits: apples emit ethylene gas which speeds up the ripening process of fruits and vegetables but has the opposite effect on potatoes, preventing them from sprouting.
**Source:** Friends of the Earth: 'Unwrapped: how throwaway plastic is failing to solve Europe's food waste problem (and what we need to do instead)', friendsoftheearth.eu

Producing a glass of dairy milk every day for a year requires 650 sq m (7,000 sq ft) of land, the equivalent of two tennis courts and more than 10 times as much as the same amount of oat milk, according to this study. Almond milk requires more water to produce than soy or oat milk. A single glass requires 74 litres (156 US pints) of water – more than a typical shower. Rice milk is also comparatively thirsty, requiring 54 litres (114 US pints) of water per glass. However, it's worth noting that both almond and rice milk still require less water to produce than the typical glass of dairy milk.
**Source:** *Science* magazine, science.sciencemag.org

> **In UK households, a weekly average of £2.40 is spent on purchases of cleaning products.**
>
> Source: www.statista.com/statistics/285609

> **A public poll found 60% would support a deposit return scheme in the UK.**
>
> Source: seas-at-risk.org

This chart is from Stroud District Council. Kerbside services may vary where you live.

# Further reading

## Books

Recipes for Natural Beauty, Romy Fraser, Neal's Yard Remedies 2007

The Art of the Natural Home: A Room by Room Guide, Rebecca Sullivan, Kyle Books, 2017

Plastic Free: How I Kicked the Plastic Habit, Beth Terry, Skyhorse Publishing, 2015

How to Give Up Plastic: Simple steps to living consciously on our blue planet, Will McCallum, Penguin Life, 2019

Turning the Tide on Plastic: How Humanity (And You) Can Make Our Globe Clean Again, Lucy Siegle, Trapeze, 2018

## Online resources

- **Action on plastic:** www.actiononplastic.org
- **Milk refill station near you:** www.beeswaxwraps.co.uk/milk-refill-map
- **Zero waste shops near you:** www.beeswaxwraps.co.uk/zero-waste-shop-map
- **Zero Waste Chef:** www.zerowastechef.com
- **Zero Waste Europe:** www.zerowasteeurope.eu
- **Living Without Plastic (Claudi Williams):** www.pfree.co.uk
- **Break Free From Plastic:** www.breakfreefromplastic.org
- **Sustainable(ish):** www.asustainablelife.co.uk
- **City to Sea:** www.citytosea.org.uk
- **Plastic Free Communities:** www.sas.org.uk/plastic-free-communities
- **Recycle Now:** www.recyclenow.com/recycling-knowledge
- **Ellen MacArthur Foundation:** www.ellenmacarthurfoundation.org/publications
- **Friends of the Earth:** policy.friendsoftheearth.uk/insight/ending-plastic-pollution-briefing
- **Surfers Against Sewage:** www.sas.org.uk/about-us/reports-publications/
- **Greenpeace:** www.greenpeace.org.uk/challenges/plastic-pollution/
- **WRAP:** www.wrap.org.uk/about-us/what-we-do/key-publications

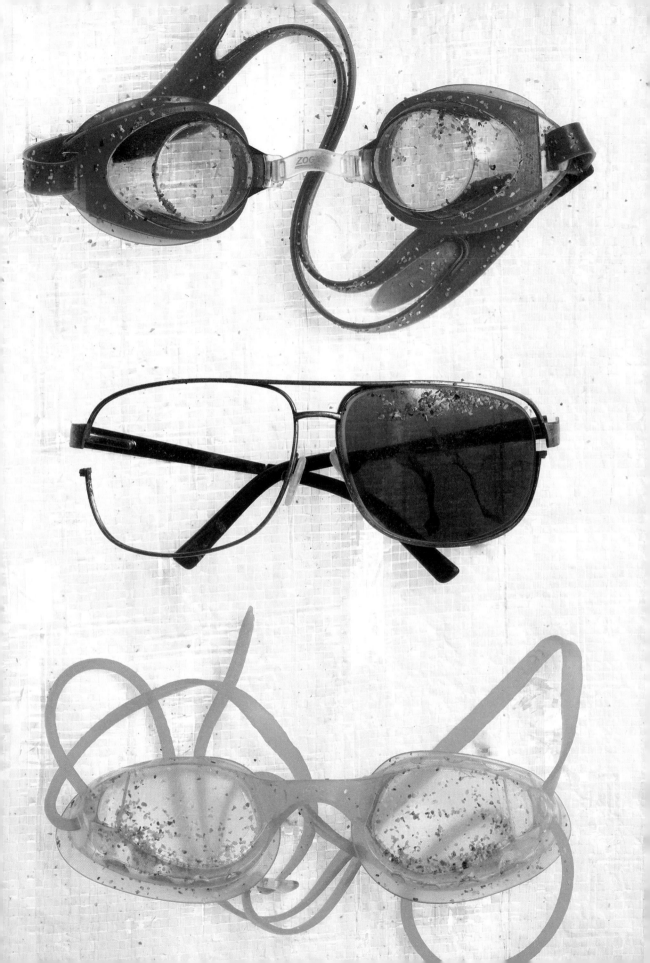

# claudi williams

A German-born, long-time resident of Stroud, Claudi is a community organiser and chair of Action on Plastic (www.actiononplastic.org), an initiative providing practical advice for individuals, businesses and communities setting out to reduce their plastic footprint. She is also the author of a blog on living without plastic (www.pfree.co.uk) and works at The Beeswax Wraps Company, a B-Corp making reusable food wraps in the UK to replace the need for clingfilm. Claudi has taken part in BBC national news and radio programmes, and has spoken at festivals, events and many local venues.

Published by Quickthorn, an imprint of Hawthorn Press Ltd.,
Hawthorn House, 1 Lansdown Lane, Stroud, Gloucestershire, GL5 1BJ
UK Tel: (01453) 757040  E-mail: info@hawthornpress.com
Website: www.hawthornpress.com

Editor: Katy Bevan
Cover shot and plastic still life images by Trudie Ballantyne @trudi_btyne
Portraits and location images by Amy Harvey @amyharveyphoto
Design and typesetting by Chris J Bailey © 2021
Printed by Cambrian Printers Ltd, Wales
Printed on Uncoated FSC® certified paper using sustainable printing procedures with a cellulose cover lamination, Cellogreen, by celloglas.co.uk

British Library Cataloging in Publication Data applied for
ISBN 978-1-912480-29-6

ACTION
ON PLASTIC

QUICK THORN

FSC
www.fsc.org

MIX
Paper from responsible sources
FSC® C004116